# Unbroken Promises

*God's Answers for the Broken Soul*

## Cheryl Clinton Weaver

**Unbroken Promises**
Copyright © 2020 Cheryl Clinton Weaver

**International Standard Book number:**
978-1-946106-56-8

**All rights reserved.**
**No part of this book may be reproduced or transmitted in any form or by any means, electronic, mechanical, including photocopying, recording, or by any information storage and retrieval system, without written permission from the author.**

Unless otherwise indicated, all Scripture quotations are taken from the King James Bible, (ASV) (Montgomery NT) (Darby) (BBE) (YLT) (NLT) (ESV) (Mace NT) (Wesley NT) (TLB). Some emphases added by author.

**Cover Design: Cheryl Clinton Weaver**
**Book Layout: Cheryl Clinton Weaver**
**Cover Art Photographer:**
Igor Zhuravlov/123RF.com

**Glorified Publishing**
**P.O. Box 8004**
**The Woodlands, TX 77387**
**www.GlorifiedPublishing.com**

**Printed in the United States of America 2020**

# ENDORSEMENTS

Sometimes spiritual words can seem vague when they don't have a 'how-to'. Cheryl has a wonderful way of explaining the 'how-to' so that the spiritual truth becomes your actual deliverance.

Kathie Walters
Www.kathiewaltersministry.com


*This book is for those ready for a swift, deep plunge into life-giving truths. It isn't for sissies, but for those who are ready to say, "bring it on." I am ready to overcome and be transformed.*

Dr. Melonie Janet Mangum, Author,
CEO Partners for Transformation,
Aglow Transformation Director


This is a great guide for anyone who has ever needed a step-by-step manual for deliverance. Believe me, this book is not just for those fresh to the faith, but for seasoned saints, too. There is no doubt that you will find yourself within the pages of Unbroken Promises. Read the book, say the prayers, and receive healing today.

Edie Bayer
Prophet, Author, Publisher
www.KingdomPromoters.org

*Rev. Cheryl Weaver has discovered that magical place where faith and fact overcome evil. Cheryl has firmly planted herself in the first rank of Christian authors. She has crafted a wildly inspirational, accurate, and intensely helpful path to defeating evil and becoming our best selves."*

*Staci McNicholl, Msw, LCSW,
Senior Therapist/Owner,
The Rock Counseling Group*

Chaplain Cheryl Weaver is a tremendously gifted woman. In my time with her, I have learned to apply God's Truth to the deep places of the heart, receive His healing, and be renewed in my mind. Not only that, but she has taught me to do the same for others. I am excited to see what God will do through her new book, "Unbroken Promises"!

Samuel Carroll,
Bible Teacher, Musician
International Students, Inc., Campus Staff
www.isionline.org

*Anyone who has ever met Apostle Cheryl Weaver is keenly aware of her love for the Lord. Cheryl's passion is contagious. She inspires all who know her to rise to new heights of worship and dedication. The authentic life she lives is communicated now in her new book, "Unbroken Promises." In every chapter of this inspirational guide to a victorious life, Cheryl ties together her real life-giving principles from the Word of God.*

*Dr. Patti Amsden
Founder, Patti Amsden Ministries and
East Gate Reformation Training Institute*


Apostle Cheryl and There's More Ministries are making an impact on many lives. All honor and praise to God! My life has been transformed through the power and presence of God through There's More Ministries. Praise the Lord for Apostle Cheryl Weaver's radical obedience and willingness to serve and sacrifice in the Ministry towards building the Kingdom of God. I am grateful for all I have learned and grown closer in my relationship with God. The Gospel of Jesus Christ is transforming people. I am a sign and a wonder. Love and Blessings,

Tanya L. White,
Chaplain, Church of God


*Apostle Cheryl Weaver is a woman under authority and reminds me of the faithful Centurion, who knows how to take orders from the Father and who knows how to delegate. I was so impressed with the spiritual maturity of those surrounding you. It's like a group of special forces, an elite team.*

*Annie McCaffrey,
Missionary*

I can never express the amount of respect and love I have for Apostle Cheryl Weaver. I'm so amazed at how much I learned from the time that we spent together. I even learn from the time that we don't spend together. I thank God he sent this blonde whirlwind into my life to blow off the ash of my faith and guide me back to a path with him. Through knowing you, I have been blessed with some of the greatest gifts one can ever receive from Jesus. I have come to know that I am worthy of love. I am learning to love people with no conditions or limits, I am learning to trust again, and most of all, I am learning that God is more real than I had ever imagined.

Jennifer James, Artist
James 222 Studios,
FB: James222Studios

*The healing Ministry of Apostle Cheryl Weaver I have received in Jesus Christ has transformed my mind, body, soul, and spirit. I did not know until the Lord revealed it to me that your soul could be healed. I didn't know how that could be done, but to ask my Father for it. Jesus ministered to me, then sent Apostle Weaver into my life to learn how to pray and walk it out. I am grateful for what God has done and continues to do in me through the healing of my soul and heart. I am thankful for the tools that He has entrusted to Apostle Weaver and her Ministry to bring others into wholeness with the Lord.*

*Misty Bullard,*
*Spiritual Daughter*

Testimony's to God's Glory! I love it when God shows up! It feels like heaven in your meetings! A beautiful display of each person has a part to share. Love, Honor, and Grace fill the room. What a visitation! The Lord is mighty to save! Bless you, Apostle Weaver.

Deborah Bobsin,
Woman of God

CHERYL CLINTON WEAVER

## DEDICATION

I dedicate this book to my mother, Betty Louise Petro Clinton, who passed away April 9th 2014 just three weeks before her 70th birthday. This is for you, Mom, the author that wasn't yet recognized. God has preserved your legacy in your daughter and granddaughter with this being the first book published in our family -- your inheritance retained. Between every chapter I have placed the poems that you wrote. You were my biggest cheerleader and you believed in us even when we couldn't believe in ourselves. This book is for you, Mom. We love you!

Betty became a licensed minister with New Life Church in Apopka, Florida.

Betty Clinton and Cassia Weaver 2001
Betty Louise Petro Clinton,
April 27th, 1944 – April 9th, 2014

# CONTENTS

| | | |
|---|---|---|
| | Endorsements | iii |
| | Dedication | ix |
| | Acknowledgments | xiii |
| | Preface | xv |
| | Prologue | xvii |
| | Introduction | xix |
| 1 | The Promise Yet to Come | 1 |
| 2 | The Promise of Intimacy | 9 |
| 3 | The Promise of Obedience | 17 |
| 4 | The Promise of Repentance | 25 |
| 5 | The Promise of Discernment, Deliverance & Power | 33 |
| 6 | The Promise of His Word | 51 |
| 7 | The Promise of Peace | 59 |
| 8 | The Promise of Forgiveness | 67 |
| 9 | The Promise of Overcoming | 87 |
| 10 | Pain & The Promise of His Presence | 103 |
| 11 | The Promises of Life | 119 |
| 12 | Perseverance to the Promise | 127 |
| | RESOURCES | 135 |

References & Citations 153

About the Author 155

# POETRY

| | | |
|---|---|---|
| 1 | Run Away, Run Away | 7 |
| 2 | If My Friends Could See Me Now | 15 |
| 3 | Trust | 23 |
| 4 | Come Reside in Me | 32 |
| 5 | The King, The Cross and Me | 49 |
| 6 | The Spirit | 57 |
| 7 | The Word Became Flesh 1 | 65 |
| 8 | The Word Became Flesh II | 86 |
| 9 | Calvary | 101 |
| 10 | This is my Lord | 117 |
| 11 | One Voice | 125 |
| 12 | God Loves Me | 134 |

## ACKNOWLEDGMENTS

It is with heartfelt gratitude that I want to say "Thank you" to Papa God for the consistent nudge to stretch me past all comfort zones to accomplish His will in writing this book. Holy Spirit, you have been my best friend and enabled me to experience so much healing and deliverance in my life. Everything I have is because of you. Thank you for loving me, Lord Jesus. One of my own quotes that I share with others applies here, "Everyone has a story to share, a part to play, and a gift to give." This is my story, my part and my gift -- first to Him and second to whom He shares it with.

Allow me to say a great big "thank you" to three precious women in my life.

To my little sister in the Spirit, Jennifer James, you have been the strength that has constantly prompted me that I am called to write and I have something to say. Thank you, Jennifer, for your love, reminders and support. Without your help this author would have never come forth.

To my friend, Lindsay, thank you for helping me to edit my words, thoughts and ideas in an understandable way for the readers. You truly are a Proverbs 31 woman, a woman of many gifts, talents, and loves. The love we share the most is that of our precious Holy Spirit. It's an honor to call you friend.

To my friend Gloria, I am humbled by your continued prophetic encouragement and your hunger for more of the

Father. Thank you for sharing your gifts and talents that have brought this project to its final completion. You are a blessing in so many ways.

Thank you to Prophetess Edie Bayer, who encourages all of us to get the Lord's word out for others to receive! You are a blessing to so many, and I appreciate all you have done to assist me in accomplishing God's will for my life, bringing this eight-year prophesied project to fruition.

To one of the strongest women I have ever met, my dear friend Beverly Hillmer. Beverly, thank you for walking me through this journey called "the Christian Life" and doing life together with me. You have walked me through many trials, healings and revelations in my life. Your faith, strength in the Word, and the depth of God you carry have seen me through so many dark moments into His marvelous light.

It is an honor to call each of you friends and sisters in Christ.

Last, and most importantly, words are not enough to convey my deepest profound love and appreciation for the man I call husband, Mr. Wayne Weaver. You have supported me in every venture, every up and down, every new idea and most of all, through all the warfare in seeing God's call manifest in my life. Thank you for gently holding my hand, my heart and most of all my love all these years. You are truly the wind beneath my wings and I thank you for your unconditional love and support of God's will in my life.

# PREFACE

Dear Reader,

It is with delight that I share my story, my training, and the Lord's amazing healing and delivering power unto Salvation.

I have been saved and in leadership since 1990. For over 30 years I have held leadership roles with multiple ministries, traveled the nations and served the Kingdom of God. I have worked in the secular marketplace as a Chaplain and served as a community Chaplain for many years. In 2005, I was ordained as a Minister and later as an Apostle.

During my years in ministry, I have personally ministered one-on-one to hundreds and hundreds of people in the areas of inner healing, deliverance, physical healing, healing from abortion, mentoring; also the salvation and maturing of individuals, teams, businesses and churches in leadership. In 2013 the Lord asked me to start There's More Ministries, Inc. and to write several books. This first book is His Story interwoven with mine. A second book on "The Abuse Structure" and how it enslaves us, then a third on "The Importance of an Apology" will follow.

It is my prayer that as you read this you will find hope, knowing you're not alone and there are promises to your problems that will prophetically advance you into your purpose!

Blessings of Great Joy,

Cheryl Weaver

www.CherylWeaver.org

**There's More Ministries, Inc.
Bringing God's Presence, Power, Precepts and
Purpose to People**

*Our Mission –*

*There's More Ministries, Inc. is a "catalyst" ministry birthing a five-fold Kingdom culture of personal restoration, church transformation and community reformation where everyone has a part to play, a story to share and a gift to give bringing God's presence, power, precepts and purpose to people.*

*There's More Ministries, Inc.
Founder: Rev. Cheryl Weaver, Five-Fold Minister, Chaplain*
P.O. Box 6801 Champaign, IL 61826
Phone: 888-850-3222
www.theresmoreministries.com
info@theresmoreministries.com

# PROLOGUE

### Acts 2:37-39 (KJV)

*[37] Now when they heard this, they were pricked in their heart, and said unto Peter and to the rest of the apostles, Men and brethren, what shall we do?*
*[38] Then Peter said unto them, Repent, and be baptized every one of you in the name of Jesus Christ for the remission of sins, and ye shall receive the gift of the Holy Ghost.*

*[39] For **the promise is unto you**, and to your children, and to all that are afar off, even as many as the Lord our God shall call.*

When I was born, my father named me Cheryl Ann, which means "beautiful one" or the "epitome of femininity and charity married with grace". On a regular basis through my life I would ask the Lord to restore me to my original design -- the plan and design for who I am to be from the beginning of time. However, we live in a very marred world with evil all around and it is easy to lose sight of His original design.

Therefore, to become an "Overcomer" we must keep our accounts short, forgive quickly, and keep our hearts pure before God. Our journey is always about TRUST. Who can we trust? When we don't believe in God, we place our trust in people and they often fail us miserably. It takes a while to wade through the murky waters of man's sins against us. Then as we get to know the Lord, have encounters with Jesus, the Holy Spirit and Papa God, we begin to grow in our trust processes with them. The Father is always providing opportunities to reveal to us that He is faithful and trustworthy.

CHERYL CLINTON WEAVER

# INTRODUCTION

THERE'S MORE -- There are promises untapped!

> "Many seek to find out how many imperfections, failures, and carnal traits are allowable in religion, but few **seek to bring Christians to the height of the gospel standard and to the unlimitations of the promises of God. The measure of the stature of the fullness** is seldom mentioned much less demonstrated, while the stature of littleness, emptiness, and powerlessness of Christianity is often emphasized and demonstrated." *Dake, Finis. Dakes Annotated Reference Bible: the Holy Bible, Containing the Old and New Testaments of the Authorized or King James Version Text. Dake Publishing, Inc., 1991, Page 214 NT, Eph. 4:12, "Seven Duties of Ministers"*

I read this outstanding note from Finis Dake in his Study Bible. It encapsulates why I have written this book and how I feel about what is missing in our Christian experience today.

**God is limitless.** We serve a limitless Creator who lives in us. He desires to provide us with everything that is written in His Word and MORE! There's always more! We are Christians: anointed beings with power to embody the fullness and wholeness of the Holy Spirit's love, power and demonstration of who Jesus is. This is all in our PERSONHOOD, OUR FLESH!

This reminds me of a saying I have about marriage. "God

created marriage before the fall and I will not settle for anything less." Jesus came and died on the Cross of Calvary to redeem us to right relationship with God the Father. That was the original intent and desire, before the fall, and still is today after the fall of Adam and Eve: fullness, wholeness, empowered with sacrificial love, wisdom, knowledge and understanding. Isaiah 11 says it well,

> *Isaiah 11:1-2 (KJV)*
>
> [1] *And there shall come forth a rod out of the stem of Jesse, and a Branch shall grow out of his roots:* [2] *And the spirit of the LORD shall rest upon him, the spirit of wisdom and understanding, the spirit of counsel and might, the spirit of knowledge and of the fear of the LORD;*

We have been restored into the promise -- the promise of fullness in Christ Jesus!

I hope as you read through the chapters of this book that you encounter the anointing of fullness as a tangible "Presence" that comes upon your life. It is the fullness I felt in God's unbroken promises through all His restoration of my brokenness. I am praying for you to receive abundantly from the Holy Spirit as you read. May the limitless resurrection power of Jesus Christ overwhelm you and may He bring you healing, revelation, and deliverance. I pray for God's deep abiding LOVE to flow through you.

Remember, the love we give away is the only love we keep!

Blessings of great Joy,
Cheryl

# Unbroken Promises

## God's Answers for the Broken Soul

CHERYL CLINTON WEAVER

## CHAPTER ONE
# THE PROMISE YET TO COME

*Jeremiah 29:11-14 (KJV)*
*11 For I know the thoughts that I think toward you, saith the LORD, thoughts of peace, and not of evil, to give you an expected end. 12 Then shall ye call upon me, and ye shall go and pray unto me, and I will hearken unto you. 13 And ye shall seek me, and find me, when ye shall search for me with all your heart.*
*14 And I will be found of you, saith the LORD: and I will turn away your captivity...*

I was about 19 years old and armed with outrageous boldness, the beginnings of a small amount of education in the tourism field and, unbeknown to me, a divine ordering of my footsteps from a God I hadn't really been introduced to yet. I read an ad in the *"Indianapolis Star"* that there was a new Union Station opening in downtown Indianapolis and there were secretarial jobs available. I jumped in the car and an hour later arrived downtown. I searched for a parking spot and started wandering around through the maze of offices until I heard people through a door. I walked in (I thought I was applying for a secretarial position) and they said, "You're here! Go over there and put in your application." There were hundreds of people everywhere! Overwhelmed and not knowing what was happening, I'm thinking "Okay?" and I obeyed instructions. So I placed my application. They interviewed me on the spot and gave me a job! They sent me through orientation and discussed what I was to wear for a uniform, and the next thing I knew I was hired as a tour guide for downtown Indianapolis Union Station's Grand

Opening! How I ended up in that room is a mystery unto God alone, resulting with a job in my chosen field. A girl from a little town in the big city with hundreds of buildings and, "Voila"! It was a Holy Spirit setup! There were more setups to come.

Let me tell you about the man with the golden necklace. **I had never met anyone like him.** He reminded me of Santa, always jolly with a big round belly. I became friends with this older, jolly black man. His name was Dan Rogers. He and I got along very well -- we clicked. We worked the front desk of the Union Station together and gave tours throughout the station.

As we worked the front desk and got to know everyone there, Dan and I developed a connection. He introduced me to his wife and they would invite me to lunch on our lunch breaks, and from time to time would purchase my meal. One afternoon, he invited me over for dinner to meet his seven children (teens to adults) and I was welcomed like one of the family. They were a family of many children to feed and, as tour guides, we only made minimum wage. I was mesmerized by his goodness and by his giving heart.

About a year later he stopped me at work and asked me, "What kind of necklace do you like when you wear a necklace? Long? Short?". Not thinking anything I said, "Long!" and went about my business. The next week he came up to me and said, "I have something for you." HE HANDED ME A BEAUTIFUL LONG GOLD NECKLACE! Now, I am a co-worker but in my mind, a total stranger. My dad never did anything that nice for me. This man who had eight mouths to feed is giving me a gold necklace? It touched me deeply! Gifts are my love language and I can probably tell you, to this day, who purchased every gift I have ever received. Looking back now as a believer, I see the signs of his faith in Jesus that came from witnessing to me through deeds of love and giving. All his family members were all believers, as I witnessed later at his funeral.

I know with all my heart that Dan Rogers is the reason that I know Jesus as my Lord and Savior today. The Word of God says that some plant the seed and some water the seed. Dan Rogers and his family planted and sowed financially, sowed family time and sowed love into a very lost and lonely girl looking for love in all the wrong places. I believe the Lord spoke to him and instructed him to purchase that necklace and that he prayed over that necklace and claimed my soul for Jesus. As I wore that necklace, I came to discover the love and promises of a true Father in heaven.

The Father knows each one of us intimately and he knows our love language. Papa God always knows how to get our attention! I always knew there was something different about that man! He passed away a couple of years after that, and I learned that He was a "man of faith" when I attended his funeral. He had touched so many people. There were hundreds of people at his "celebration of life" that day. Looking back and knowing what I know now, I realize it was that golden necklace that was prayed over that I wore daily for years that led me and guided my path right into salvation's doorway.

GOD is faithful, and Dan Rogers was faithful at his own expense to share with me his time, his love, his family, his money, his supper table and his prayerful golden necklace. I will never forget how this man touched me so deeply. It wasn't until five years later, after a mental breakdown and an audible voice from God, that I walked across the threshold to know that God was real. But the day of the golden gift was the day I was marked with a price, a sacrificial gift from the sower, for the great harvest of a seed. God is faithful and we are called to be His faithful servants.

***1 Corinthians 4:2 (Wesley NT)***
*² Moreover it is required in stewards that a man be found faithful.*

***1 Corinthians 1:9 (Wesley NT)***
*9 God is faithful, by whom ye were called into the fellowship of his Son Jesus Christ our Lord.*

In sharing this story of my journey I am reminded of the story of Stephen in the Bible and how Stephen was a sacrificial seed. My paraphrased version: Saul (Paul) was a zealous Pharisee and he did everything to the letter of the law. In other words, Paul was super religious. He was so zealous that he felt it was his godly duty (obviously misdirected) to kill all the Jesus followers. Saul was tormenting and killing believers right after Jesus had died on the Cross. Stephen, on the other hand, was a devoted follower of Jesus. As Stephen was being stoned to death by Saul he also, like Jesus, said as he was dying, "Lord, forgive them, for they do not know what they are doing." Stephen became the seed for Saul's conversion. As Stephen became the sacrificial lamb, his seed died and went into the ground and produced a harvest. The harvest was Saul's soul being converted to Paul who became a believer in Christ Jesus. He was saved. The Word says: be imitators of Me; pick up your cross; and, love not your life unto death.

***Acts 7:59-60 (BBE)***
*⁵⁹ And Stephen, while he was being stoned, made prayer to God, saying, Lord Jesus, take my spirit.*
*⁶⁰ And going down on his knees, he said in a loud voice, Lord, do not make them responsible for this sin. And when he had said this, he went to his rest.*

***1 Corinthians 4:16 (ASV)***
*16 I beseech you therefore, be ye imitators of me.*

***Mark 10:21 (Mace NT)***

*21 then Jesus looking upon him with a favorable eye, said, there is one thing still to be done; go, sell all your estate, and give it to the poor, and you shall have treasure in heaven; then come, take up the Cross, and follow me.*

### Revelation 12:11 (KJV)
*11 And they overcame him by the blood of the Lamb, and by the word of their testimony; and they loved not their lives unto the death.*

### 1 Corinthians 3:6-9 (BBE)
*6 I did the planting, Apollos did the watering, but God gave the increase. 7 So then the planter is nothing, and the waterer is nothing; but God who gives the increase. 8 Now the planter and the waterer are working for the same end: but they will have their separate rewards in the measure of their work. 9 For we are workers with God: you are God's planting, God's building.*

### John 4:34-36 (KJV)
*[34] Jesus saith unto them, My meat is to do the will of him that sent me, and to finish his work.*
*35 Say not ye, There are yet four months, and then cometh harvest? behold, I say unto you, Lift up your eyes, and look on the fields; for they are white already to harvest.*
*36 And he that reapeth receiveth wages, and gathereth fruit unto life eternal: that both he that soweth and he that reapeth may rejoice together.*

Even before we know the Lord, He knows us! He created you in your mother's womb, designed you before the foundation of the earth and destined you to be here with His purpose and promise. He loves us with an everlasting love and wants to lavish His love upon us. His promises are ours if we will believe and yield to a better, more glorious way beyond our own understanding!

*Psalm 37:4-5 (KJV)*
4 Delight thyself also in the LORD; and he shall give thee the desires of thine heart.
5 Commit thy way unto the LORD; trust also in him; and he shall bring it to pass.

**Prayer Point**

**Prayer: Dear Lord Jesus, I believe you are the Son of God. I believe you died on the Cross a sinless man; that you were born of the Virgin Mary as God and man. You paid the price for my sins on the Cross by taking my punishment for me. I ask forgiveness for my sins. I invite you into my heart as Lord and Savior. Amen.**

Note: There is a scriptural resource called <u>The Romans Road</u> in the *Resources & Helps* section at the back of this book. If you have never invited Jesus into your life, I encourage you to pray this prayer of salvation and then ask Jesus to reveal Himself to you. He will! Be sure to tell us you invited Jesus into your heart!

## RUN AWAY, RUN AWAY

I LEFT MY LIFE TODAY, I WENT AWAY
I ASK YOU NOW HOW MY SOUL CAN BE
LIKE RAZOR-SHARP GLASS BROKEN
AND SHATTERED INSIDE OF ME
SO AS I PICK UP THE PIECES I SEE
MY FINGERS ARE COVERED
IN THE BLOOD OF THOSE EXPECTATIONS OF ME
I TRIED TO TELL, I HOPED ALL WOULD SEE
BUT ALAS ,IT WAS NOT TO BE
NOW I'M CONSUMED IN THE PRESSURE-COOKER
OF EXPECTATIONS OF ME
WHAT DO YOU SAY TO THOSE
WHOSE LOVE EXPECTS EVER MORE
THAN YOU THINK OR HOPE YOU CAN BE
IT LOOKS AS IF EXPECTATIONS HAVE
PLACED ME RIGHT INTO A BOX
A DARK AND SMALL PLACE, YOU SEE
AND EVERY TIME I TRY TO PUSH
OUT INTO THE LIGHT SO I CAN BREATHE
EXPECTATIONS COME HUNTING FOR ME
THEN RIGHT BACK INTO THE BOX I GO
NEVER ENOUGH LIGHT TO SEE
NOT ENOUGH TO STAY & BELIEVE
RUN AWAY, RUN AWAY
IS THE VOICE THAT SCREAMED AT ME
DAY AFTER DAY, GET AWAY, GET AWAY
BUT NOW, I AM HERE AT LAST WHERE

## CHERYL CLINTON WEAVER

NO ONE EXPECTS ANYTHING FROM ME
AND YET THE VOICES INSIDE STILL SCREAM
RUN AWAY, RUN AWAY, GET AWAY, BE FREE
I LEFT ALL EXPECTATIONS BEHIND ME
SO WHY DOES IT SEEM EXPECTATIONS
STILL SURROUND AND CONFOUND ME
WHAT DO I SAY TO THE BURDENED SOUL
I CARRY AROUND THAT LIVES INSIDE OF ME
DARE I LOOK MORE CLOSELY INSIDE, DARE I SEE
IT IS MY OWN EXPECTATIONS THAT HAVE BEEN
THE BREAKING OF ME

Matthew 11: 29-30

Betty Clinton
March 2005

## CHAPTER TWO
# THE PROMISE OF INTIMACY

Have you ever just sat and longed to be known? Longed for a time just to be known by someone in the very depths of your being? That someone would just know who you really are and why you exist and what your desires are. That kind of knowing is a longing for intimacy that is not easily found in person-to- person connections without a secret ingredient -- the Creator Himself. He designed us, you and me, with that deep desire to need to be needed, need to be known, and need to be loved to the core of our beings. WHY, you ask? Well, because **GOD Himself wants to be known by you and wants to provide you with the deepest intimacy that you will ever experience in this lifetime – Himself.**

Intimacy flourished in a special time and place with someone you love, whether it's a close friend, a sister or you're betrothed. There is a special way that someone you're intimate with touches in your soul. It's more than just a fleshly touch or an emotional embrace, it's a "deep calls unto deep" love connection that reaches into the depths of our souls. We often think as humans that we are the author of such connections. We choose to let others in and therefore it's us in control, and to some extent we do participate in the equation. However, I believe we moved far deeper means than just our outward experiences in this life. We are connected to the Creator of the Universe and He is most definitely connected to us. We are spiritual beings that He has created. He has designed us with this profound need to be deeply known.

God provides true satisfaction, deep contentment and fullness of love -- abounding, unlimited, vast and free. He has this kind of affectionate relationship with those who ask, just because they ask! He longs for us, as we long in our soul's unmet need, until we discover the fullness of His love towards us. And when we allow Him to meet that need – WOW! Then our beings begin to come into order, other relationships start coming into alignment and our love meter becomes full, not demanding toward others. We become generous souls. It becomes a loosing of what we have received from Him. We can now freely give vast, deep, and unquenchable love because we have received it freely from our Father through His Son, Jesus.

In 1988, I had just come home from a bar and I had been through three broken relationships. I was done with love, men and having a shattered heart. I decided I was going to close my heart down; never again would I allow anyone to hurt me. "I will lock my heart down behind a vault with chains and padlocks." At that very moment, when I was about to make that decision, I read a plaque on my wall (it jumped out at me) that said, "*The love we give away, is the only love we keep.*". In a loud, audible voice I heard the Lord speak to me. "TRUST ME", He said, and I knew that HE didn't want me to lock my heart down. He wanted me to continue to love and trust. I thought to myself, "Whoa! God is REAL! I guess I'd better find a church!".

That was the beginning of my journey to having that deep longing in my soul find fulfilled and be rest. I started to feel the intimacy of a Father reaching down into my heart, feeding me and healing my soul. That day was the beginning of the greatest love affair of my life. My heart aches now when I haven't spent enough time with my heavenly Father. I long to be in His presence and He longs to be in mine. As the maiden states in the Bible, in the Book of Song of Songs, "I am His Beloved and He is mine.".

I spent night after night searching for that longing to be filled with men, sex, lust, affections, flirtations, dancing -- anything that would create a "high" that said to my heart, "You are needed, significant, special, loved.". Man after man, sex partner after sex partner, it slowly just continued to diminish me little by little and I became more and more empty. That's why the scripture says in Hebrews 11:25, *"Sin is pleasurable for a time…"* and in Romans 6:23, *"The wages of sin is death."*

Unfortunately, like all addictions, more and more is required to fill the emptiness inside the addict. It is a vicious cycle of debauchery that steals the very essence of who you truly are; you trade your soul for some empty, artificial ray of love and affection to fill the void, but fulfillment NEVER COMES. There is never a point of true satisfaction, just more shattered fragments.

**We never receive fulfillment when we are taking from someone else.** The enemy steals, he is a thief, and the bible says in John 10:10, "He comes to steal, kill and destroy.". If we have never received the fullness of God's relationship through His Son Jesus Christ and invited Him into our heart and soul, turning away from our old life, then we are destined to serve Satan. Satan's agenda is simple -- to destroy you mind, body and soul.

When we walk in the characteristics of GOD we receive the benefits of that walk. When we are looking for some person to fill our need, we are taking from them. Co-dependency is giving by taking. That was the family environment that surrounded me and the many generations before me. As I started into counseling, the question that brought my "aha" moment was, "Cheryl, what is the common denominator in all these broken relationships?" "ME!" I said. That was a hard day but one of great revelation. A change came forth in my will that day.

When situations you're in with person after person always end up with the same results, the common denominator is you! Well, that hit me right between the eyes! But God used it to thrust me towards my journey of healing, learning and growing, and eventually opened my understanding to see the love of my heavenly Father. His love fueled in me an insatiable appetite for truth. That is when I met the Author of Truth, GOD the Father. His audible voice stopped and protected me from making the worst mistake of my life -- choosing a cold, locked down heart! That was the beginning of my introduction. It would take another 24 months before I was fully introduced to Jesus as Lord and Savior officially.

What is it like, intimacy with the King of Kings, the Father of my heart and the Lover of my soul? My heart is full of peace. My heart is full of joy. My heart is full of the deepest, unquenchable love – love I have never found in a human person. **His love never leaves you;** a love that never disappoints you and a love that fulfills you to the greatest heights, lengths, depths and breadths. **His love is limitless towards us!** You can't outgive God. His love was first reflected towards us by placing His Son on a cross to die for us so that we would be able to receive His love for all eternity, instead of the vast penalty we deserve -- judgment of our sin, which is the punishment I deserved for breaking the commandments of God's Word and standards by walking in fornication, lust, perversions, and sexual sins. He loves us so much HE made a way of escape from that judgment -- His name is Jesus Christ, God's only begotten Son, born of God (supernatural, supreme Creator) and born of Mary (humanity).

Jesus made the way of escape through the Cross, which provided the final sacrifice for sin so that Father could look upon us as "justified" through the blood that was shed. This means that our Father in heaven promises to be in relationship with us "just as though we had never sinned" because Jesus took our punishment upon Himself as an innocent lamb being led to the slaughter for all humanity, for all eternity -- our evil sins being placed upon Him at that very moment in time. Why? To restore intimacy and relationship as it was intended to be before the fall of Adam and Eve.

Abba Father desires relationship, family and, most important, love. In the book of John it says, "God is Love". Without Him we don't know what love truly is. Without understanding the truest form and definition of love, we cannot bestow real love upon others. God sent Jesus to fill that void in our souls. God sent Jesus to restore the promise of walking with Him in the cool of the day. God sent Jesus for us to truly know Him. God sent Jesus to understand that we are known by Him.

I had started my journey towards learning that, "The love we give away is the only love we keep."

**Prayer Point**

**Dear Lord Jesus, come and fill me. I want to feel Your love, the love Jesus paid the price for. I want more of You. Help me to let go of all my guards, walls and self-protection. Help me trust You more. I surrender my fear. I give You permission, Holy Spirit, to come deeper into my soul. I receive in, Jesus' name. Amen.**

Note: In the *Resource and Helps* section there is a special prayer to receive a special impartation of the Baptism of the Holy Spirit. The Holy Spirit fills us with God Himself, empowering us with more love, joy, peace, patience, kindness, gentleness,

faithfulness and self-control. He also gives us many gifts like healing, wisdom, discernment and much more.
(It is like the gas in the tank that makes the car run.)

## *IF MY FRIENDS COULD SEE ME NOW*

If my friends could see me now
What a surprise I would be
Turned around, born anew
Forsaking my yesterdays
As I give myself to You

If my friends could see me now
With this glow on my face
Your song of love on my lips
And a smile in my heart
For no one but You

If my friends could see me now
They would see but a reflection
Of your grace and purity
For as I lay myself down
You guide me into maturity

If my friends could see me now
They would see me loving You
Giving all that I am
Heart, soul and spirit
While gaining divine liberty

If my friends could see me now
I would say but one thing
He knows you and loves you perfectly
So now is the time, do not delay
If you will but ask, He gives life eternally

*Betty Clinton*
*July 1999*

CHERYL CLINTON WEAVER

## CHAPTER THREE
# THE PROMISE OF OBEDIENCE

There is a scripture I like to say to myself from time to time, "...and forget not all his benefits.". Did you know that when we serve, obey and love the Lord, receiving Jesus as Savior, it comes with a benefits package? There are hidden gems in the sea of real life; stories of soldiers, fisherman, prophets, sheep herdsman, prostitutes, and mothers. There in the midst of some of the most dramatic human stories ever told are awesome promises that the GOD of the Universe loves you, and provides you with benefits for serving in His Kingdom.

Like all kingdoms, there is a King and a dominion to rule. But unlike all the kings of the world, this King reigns in a different Kingdom and a different world -- the world of the hearts of men! He has come and paid a ransom price to reign over the forces of evil, to provide you with everlasting peace, love, joy, patience, kindness, goodness, gentleness, and self-control. **There is no greater authority or power than the Blood of Jesus ruling and reigning in the Kingdom of Good News.** His Kingdom will have no end, and the fruit of your obedience in this Kingdom will supply you a life of eternal rest and a source of peace, joy, and comfort here on the earth.

A special thought from a refrigerator magnet that a counselor friend once shared with me said, "Our perception is our reality.". Maybe it's our perception of obedience or what the word conjures up, even more than the act. Maybe it's our viewpoint of what we believe about the subject that filters out the benefits before we even get a chance to see the results. Maybe it's a bad experience with an abusive authority.

The first thought that comes to mind is "NO" when we hear the word obedience! We are a rebellious culture by nature. Our state of being before we knew Christ was rebellious flesh that had to die to its selfish ways daily. We know that obedience creates demands, that it requires demands toward someone we may or may not like, and often can conjure up feelings that aren't usually pleasant.

However, we like the fruit of obedience, don't we? We have more money in our accounts when we don't break the speed limit or we get an "A" on a test because we were obedient to study. Why do we avoid obedience, yet expect others to follow it? We don't want someone to run the stop sign or steal from us, yet we all struggle at times with the concept of pure and total surrender to the declared rules of the environment in which we live.

The greatest benefit is to find out that in everything you have done in your life (including every bad, evil, and disparaging thing that you may have done), this King loves you anyway. He Loves You! The love from this King comes **_unconditionally_**. You cannot earn it, create it, or buy it even though people have tried. There is nothing you can do or not do to receive this King's love. He is like the Father we always wished we'd had. He loves His children no matter what. Whether we obey him or disobey His commands, He loves us.

He loves us so much that He gave us the choice to love or not to love Him back. The Creator of the Universe, who created you and me, formed us to have a free will to choose who we would serve; ourselves, Satan, or our heavenly Father. It's really unbelievable that GOD, who created everything, wanted to give us the opportunity and free will to decide who we would serve. He loves us that much! And He provides us with a set of promises; a set of guidelines that we can follow so we will not stumble or harm ourselves. It's like getting a new car. How many of us would drive a new car off the lot and not read the instruction manual? Or put water in the gas tank? Or sit in the truck and expect it to go somewhere without knowing how to operate it? Since He created us, the Lord knew ahead of time what would cause us great harm and devastation if we chose it; so He made a way of escape through one of two roads, **obedience** or **repentance**.

The easiest way to learn something new is to find out what others have done before us and learn from their mistakes. Thomas Edison tried making a light bulb over 10,000 times. Lincoln failed his first election. Many can learn obedience by accepting what others say about a situation. The Bible is a compilation of people who have gone before us and shared their stories; it is a tremendous benefit and resource of God speaking directly to His children about what will bring blessing to our lives and overturn curses. What can bless you and all your future generations? The promises in God's Word! What can curse you and your generations? The lack of knowing God's word and laws and obeying them. The Bible says, "My people perish for lack of knowledge.".

It's all choice. What choices do you want to make? Drive down the road too fast and you will pay the fine, or we can learn from the hotrod pulled over on the side of the road receiving a ticket. God's word is for us in the same way pack-n-plays and gates are for toddlers. Why do we place children in car seats and baby proof our houses? To keep our children safe and to protect them. They do not know what can cause them harm. The King of Kings has sent his Word to help us be obedient and receive "truth". His truth brings us out of darkness and into His marvelous light. His truth brings us out of harmful practices, cycles and behaviors. As a Christian we **will** learn obedience. God will first speak to us directly, and again He will often repeat what He has said. Then if we haven't listened, He will send a prophet to confirm what He has spoken, and again He may send another prophet. If we still haven't responded, then He will send us into the wilderness to teach us how to be obedient through difficult circumstances.

The greatest gift we can give back to the Father, the King of Creation, is our obedience to unconditionally love Him back; trusting in what He says and responding to that with our acts of obedience. Obedience is FAITH in action. It says to God, "I trust You, I love You and will follow Your instructions". The Book of James says it like this,

> ***James 2:22 (KJV)***
>
> *"You see that his faith and his actions were working together, and his faith was made complete by what he did."*

There was a time in my life where I struggled with surrendering to obedience in a specific area -- the area of having a child. The Lord began testing my heart and allowing me to think I was pregnant, over and over again, for an eight year period of time. Each time I became less and less obstinate and more sensitive to what Abba Father wanted for my life. He knew more than I, and He knew the tremendous blessings that lay ahead; blessings for my future daughter, myself, the ministry and generations to come.

After eight years I said, "Lord, I will have a child out of obedience to You." I had finally overcome my unbelief. By that time in my walk with Him I knew I could trust the Lord. It was a great season of dying to my flesh and surrendering my selfish ways; laying down my life, and making my body a living sacrifice of praise, just as the Lord laid down His life for mine.

Obedience is better than sacrifice it says in 1 Samuel in the bible. There are great treasures stored up for those who walk in obedience to the Lord. Many catastrophes can be averted as we learn to listen to His still, small voice and walk in the way we are instructed by the Holy Spirit. If we are only good people, doing good deeds, sacrificing our time and resources, and are not saved and completely surrendered to Him, "it profits a man not", the bible says. If we go around doing good, but we are not being obedient to what the Lord has instructed, then our sacrifice is also wasted. It is only our sacrifices that are surrendered in obedience to our call or instruction by Holy Spirit that merits treasure laid up and stored in heaven. Our deeds are worthless and our efforts futile if our hearts are not purely connected to the Author of our faith and the Creator of our soul, serving Him in timely obedience. When we respond to Christ **immediately, radically, sacrificially, and obediently**, that is when the promises come ALIVE and we walk in increasing levels of fullness, blessing and great reward! You can never outgive God. What you give in obedience, you will reap in a fruitful harvest.

When faith is married to our **immediacy, radicalness, costliness (self-sacrifice), and obedience** there is a synergistic outpouring of heaven's responses to your sacrifice. The Kingdom of God is always about fullness and increase. He must increase so we will decrease. When we die, it is to gain. It is the same in principle when we surrender; the Lord will always out bless our giving. In fact, the only scripture in the whole bible where God says "test me" is about this concept. He is discussing your substance (your giving) and He is saying, "I will open the heavens and pour out abundance back to you.".

> *Mal. 3:10 (NLT)* "Bring all the tithes* into the storehouse so there will be enough food in my Temple. If you do," says the LORD of Heaven's Armies, "I will

*open the windows of heaven for you. I will pour out a blessing so great you won't have enough room to take it in! Try it! Put me to the test!"* *(1ˢᵗ 10% of your giving)*

In conclusion, the truth of moving in all four characteristics (**immediacy, radicalness, costliness, obedience**) births the greatest treasures of the Kingdom; blessings of abundance in every area and fullness of resurrection Life! That far outweighs sacrifice, don't you think?

**Prayer Point**

**Dear Lord Jesus, I repent of my rebellion and the rebellion of my bloodlines. I repent of my fear. I ask for Your forgiveness. I choose to forgive them. I forgive myself. I ask for Your grace (unmerited favor to enable me) to submit to Your will and walk in obedience. I ask for my faith to be awakened to serve You. Help me hear Your voice, Lord, and respond. Amen.**

## *TRUST*

My child,
trust in me,
I am your guiding light
I am to you as water to a garden
Believe in me and you shall flower and grow
I am everlasting
Father, Son and Holy Ghost
I would guide, not control you
Treasure, not own you
I will lead you only over paths
That lead to the one true peace
I am the Breath that gave you life
I am the Blood that gave you sustenance
I am the Love that gave you heart
I am the Door, the Way, and the Life
There is only one Truth
Know Me and you know the face of Love
Love unbinding and eternal
You are My child and I believe in you
Your tears are My rain
Your heartbreak, My sorrow
Your pain, My burden
Give over these things to Me
So together we may walk a path of
Unheralded peace, love and happiness

*Betty Clinton*
*September 26, 1998*

# CHERYL CLINTON WEAVER

## CHAPTER FOUR
# THE PROMISE OF REPENTANCE

The entire essence of our Kingdom relationship hinges on one truth -- **repentance.**

I am a woman of repentance! I was born on the 19th and the number 19 means repentance. I grew up in a Catholic church and every week repentance was emphasized in the receiving of the Eucharist, or simply put, Communion: a time of receiving a wafer symbolizing and representing the Body of Jesus and what He did for us by receiving all our sin, misdeeds, and moral failures on Himself -- a pardon from the coming consequences of our sin on that coming day of judgment that every man, woman, and child faces upon passing from this life into eternal life. **The most important question you'll be asked, that one decision in this lifetime that will determine your fate and future for all eternity, is –** "_**Did you receive and believe what my Son Jesus did for you on the Cross?**_"

I did receive Jesus as Savior and Lord in 1990. It was the best promise I have ever received in my entire life! I received communion with a living God who loves me dearly and wants to bless me here and now, for all eternity. It is not by working harder, performing more, helping more, or serving, BUT BY ACCEPTING AND REPENTING THAT THE PROMISE IS ACTIVATED! Are we going to refuse the free gift of pardon for our sins and reject Jesus' suffering for our sin, spending this life and the rest of our eternal life in a perpetual separation from Him who is good, loving and caring towards us?

It's a choice that faces every human soul. Repentance is the ability to lower ourselves (let go of our rights, pride, and entitlements) in our own eyes and humble ourselves in others' eyes. We do this so that we can have a clean heart and pure hands before an ever loving Father who offers us the choice of eternal life in His love. It IS worth it -- I PROMISE!

One of the biggest devastations of my life was having an abortion at the age of 18. "It is my right as a woman!" I declared proudly and was programmed by society to believe. I clung tightly to the myth, "It's only a blob of tissue.". WOW! That was the biggest lie I have ever swallowed in my entire life!

Naivety, fear, and selfishness will cause just about anyone to do anything. This is why it is so important to know that the "TRUTH" of God's Word is powerful enough to set you free! As I became more intimate with my Savior Jesus, and my Father in heaven, I became ever more aware that this decision I thought was my "right" was so wrong and so twisted. It was my God-given purpose and destiny as a woman to bring forth **LIFE**, give birth and be a nurturer of that life. The enemy of our soul (Satan) doesn't want anyone to fulfill their God-given destiny because it will cause damage to his (Satan's) kingdom.

After uncovering layers of lies and deceit that I believed, I came face-to-face with the cold reality that I had "MURDERED MY BABY". It was my hardest failure to overcome. However, once you see the truth through a loving Father's eyes, repentance comes easily. You know you are forgiven. It's forgiving yourself that then becomes the challenge of the soul. If God in heaven has chosen to forgive us our sin, who are we to say it is unforgivable?

Repentance allows you to see yourself as you truly are. The bible says the heart is deceitfully wicked.

### Jeremiah 17:9 (KJV)
*⁹ The heart is deceitful above all things, and desperately wicked: who can know it?*

Very rarely are we truly able to see ourselves as we are, without the Lord's conviction. This time of reflection is the moment of repentance. It comes through the illumination of a Savior's love for you as He draws you to see the vast need you have in your soul. You and I, and the collective people of creation, are completely void of the fullness of truth, light, and love until we meet the Lover of our soul, Jesus Christ our personal Savior, Deliverer, and Redeemer.

### John 6:44 (Montgomery NT)
*⁴⁴ answered Jesus; "no one can come to me unless the Father who sent me draw him; then I will raise him up on the last day.*

The Father never meant for us to live devoid of Him. He created us with a vacuum in our soul that only He could fill. Being a loving Father and not wanting us to be controlled by Him, He provided us with a free will and the choice to choose to love Him; the choice to receive the free gifts and promises He has provided for us. There are over 7,000 promises in the Word of God that He has provided to help us. **His promises are never broken!** If we feel that we haven't seen His promise manifest the way we expected, the error always lies with us. There's usually a lack of Kingdom knowledge (Hosea 4:6) to receive the promise. Many promises are conditional upon our obedience and/or our response to Him. He wants us to have heaven here on earth, now! The Scripture says, "He is a God that cannot lie and that He is the same yesterday, today and tomorrow. That His promises are "yes and amen," (paraphrased) and if you have already broken the laws of God like I had, He will forgive you and redeem your brokenness through Jesus' shed blood. This restores us back to receiving His promises!

I repented that day after my revelation of, "I murdered my baby." It was a very ugly, disgusting, and repulsive thing to look at -- still to this day the ugliest I have ever seen in myself. That is SIN. No matter how big or small we see it, all sin is measured the same: EVIL. Sin is filthy, it's repulsive, abhorrent and foul. It is evil! **Yet God** in all His mercy reached down into creation by sending Himself (Jesus) to be born of a human (100 percent God and 100 percent man) to repudiate my sin, receiving it upon His son IN MY PLACE. As I began to trust in His love for me, I received His love. As I received His love, I trusted when He said, "I forgive you" -- He forgives! It's like when you try and hold a beach ball underwater. Every cell in my being was holding that secret down like that beach ball under water. Every molecule of my being was holding down the pain, guilt, shame, death, murder, heartlessness, and rage that I had carried for seven years. It was all <u>released that day</u>! The weights, burdens, and demons that were tormenting me -- gone! I could breathe again and experience deeper feelings of the Father's abiding love that I hadn't known on earth. I was forgiven!! I was guilt free!! The Bible says that, "He forgives us and puts our sin away as far as the east is from the west, never to be remembered any more!". I WAS FREE!!

> ***Hebrews 8:12 (Montgomery NT)***
> *¹² For I will have mercy upon their wrong-doings, and their sins I will remember no more."*
>
> ***Hebrews 10:17 (Montgomery NT)***
> *¹⁷ Then he adds, and their sins and their iniquities will I remember no more.*
>
> ***Psalm 103:12 (BBE)***
> *¹² As far as the east is from the west, so far has he put our sins from us.*

**Psalm 103:12 (KJV)**
*¹² As far as the east is from the west, so far hath he removed our transgressions from us.*

That is the free gift of PARDON. Jesus provided Himself as an innocent sacrifice being crucified on the Cross to give to each one who will receive this pardon. All we have to do is humble ourselves and ask forgiveness.

**Psalm 34:18 (KJV)**
*¹⁸ The LORD is nigh unto them that are of a broken heart; and saveth such as be of a contrite spirit.*

**Psalm 51:17 (KJV)**
*¹⁷ The sacrifices of God are a broken spirit: a broken and a contrite heart, O God, thou wilt not despise.*

What is true, holy repentance? It is a time of utterly understanding that you, as a human being, have made a grave and grievous error against God. There is only one source that can restore you, one pardon that can redeem that error, the shed Blood of Jesus Christ.

Webster's dictionary states: ¹Repent means to turn from sin and dedicate oneself to the amendment of one's life and/or to feel regret or contrition; the actions of repenting for misdeeds or moral shortcomings. Why is it necessary to repent or admit our failures and wrong doings? Why not simply push them down into the cavern we call a psyche and repress them? Well, like a beach ball that someone tries to hold under water, it requires much strain and continued pressure to persist in keeping that ball under the water. So it is with sin. It feels good for a season but always brings consequences with it.

***James 1:15 (ASV)***
*$^{15}$ Then the lust, when it hath conceived, beareth sin: and the sin, when it is full grown, bringeth forth death.*

Repentance is like drinking a tall glass of ice-cold water after a long day outside in the hot sun with nothing to drink all day. The Word says that, as we repent, our sins are no longer remembered or recorded in heaven against us and that there comes a due season of revival, a recovery of fresh breath, and a time of refreshing and cleansing of the soul.

***Acts 3:19 (Montgomery NT) TURN***
*$^{19}$ "Repent then! And reform, from the blotting out of your sins, so that there may come times of refreshing from the presence of the Lord;*

***Acts 3:19 (KJV)***
*$^{19}$ Repent ye therefore, and be converted, that your sins may be blotted out, when the times of refreshing shall come from the presence of the Lord;*

Repentance is the way to open your soul to new realms of healing, breakthrough, revelation, and conversations with the Creator of the Universe, the King of Kings, and the Lord of Lords who wants to communicate with you! He is a holy, pure, and just God and must condemn all sin. As we repent and receive Jesus Christ into our hearts, we are covered by the blood Jesus shed on the Cross. With that comes His righteousness and His justification, meaning we are "just as if we never sinned". We have been justified by the redeeming Blood of Jesus as He suffered on the Cross for us, paying the price for our sin. Now we are made whole and righteous in God's sight. We are qualified by the Blood of Jesus. It is truly that simple. It is not by works, but by BELIEVING His promise, that we receive a Divine Exchange!

***1 Peter 3:18 (YLT)***
*$^{18}$ because also Christ once for sin did*

*suffer--righteous for unrighteous--that he might lead us to God, having been put to death indeed, in the flesh, and having been made alive in the spirit,*

**Romans 5:19 (KJV)**
¹⁹ *For as by one man's disobedience many were made sinners, so by the obedience of one shall many be made righteous.*

Prayer Point

Dear Lord Jesus, reveal my heart and expose my soul. (Wait on the Holy Spirit to reveal what you need to repent of.)

I repent of _____. I renounce all demonic associations with these sins. I break all bondages associated with these behaviors. I ask for Your grace to turn from my wicked ways. I choose to submit to God, resist the enemy, and he will flee in Jesu's name. I choose to forgive myself. Thank You for Your grace and forgiveness. Amen.

## COME RESIDE IN ME

Holy Spirit, reveal Lord Jesus to me
Holy Spirit, my joy abounds in Thee
Holy Spirit, now today live in me
Holy Spirit, my strength I find in Thee
Holy Spirit, Your peace refreshes me
Holy Spirit, my trust lies in Thee
Holy Spirit, Your love surrounds me
Holy Spirit, my life depends on Thee
Holy Spirit, Holy Spirit, come reside in me

*Betty I. Clinton*
*March 29, 1999*

## CHAPTER FIVE
# THE PROMISE OF DISCERNMENT, DELIVERANCE AND POWER

Psalms 91 was my daily bread for many years. It is power! Read it declaratively.

> ***Psalm 91:1-16 (KJV)***
> *¹ He that dwelleth in the secret place of the most high shall abide under the shadow of the Almighty.*
>
> *² I will say of the LORD, He is my refuge and my fortress: my God; in him will I trust.*
>
> *³ Surely he shall deliver thee from the snare of the fowler, and from the noisome pestilence.*
>
> *⁴ He shall cover thee with his feathers, and under his wings shalt thou trust: his truth shall be thy shield and buckler.*
>
> *⁵ Thou shalt not be afraid for the terror by night; nor for the arrow that flieth by day;*
>
> *⁶ Nor for the pestilence that walketh in darkness; nor for the destruction that wasteth at noonday.*
>
> *⁷ A thousand shall fall at thy side, and ten thousand at thy right hand; but it shall not come nigh thee.*
>
> *⁸ Only with thine eyes shalt thou behold and see the reward of the wicked.*

*⁹ Because thou hast made the LORD, which is my refuge, even the most High, thy habitation;*

*¹⁰ There shall no evil befall thee, neither shall any plague come nigh thy dwelling.*

*¹¹ For he shall give his angels charge over thee, to keep thee in all thy ways.*

*¹² They shall bear thee up in their hands, lest thou dash thy foot against a stone.*

*¹³ Thou shalt tread upon the lion and adder: the young lion and the dragon shalt thou trample under feet.*

*¹⁴ Because he hath set his love upon me, therefore will I deliver him: I will set him on high, because he hath known my name.*

*¹⁵ He shall call upon me, and I will answer him: I will be with him in trouble; I will deliver him, and honour him.*

*¹⁶ With long life will I satisfy him, and shew him my salvation.*

Spiritual discernment is defined in the dictionary as: the ability to see, feel, and perceive the atmosphere around you; to discern between good and evil; and, the ability to judge well.

Fundamentally, we must understand the source from which the discernment is coming. The enemy can mimic the gifts of God. Therefore, it is important to test the spirits like 1 John 4 teaches.

**1 John 4: 1-4**
*"Beloved, do not believe every spirit, but*

> *test the spirits to see whether they are from God, because many false prophets have gone out into the world. 2By this you know the Spirit of God: every spirit that confesses that Jesus Christ has come in the flesh is from God; 3and every spirit that does not confess Jesus is not from God; this is the spirit of the antichrist, of which you have heard that it is coming, and now it is already in the world."*

There were two trees in the Garden of Eden: the Tree of Life and the Tree of the Knowledge of Good and Evil. The Spirit of Life draws from the Tree of Life. Demonic powers operate within the Tree of the Knowledge of Good and Evil. Satan cannot create, he is a created being and he can only counterfeit what God is doing. Satanic forces draw their power from the knowledge of the earthly realms and evil portals; demonic forces that have roamed the earth since the fall in the garden. They exchange information with one another through demonic networks and hierarchies. Satan was removed from the third heaven and was cast down to the first (and second) heaven where God gave mankind the command to take dominion and rule. (Gen 1:26)

Allow me to lay a foundation of understanding of the heavens to proceed. The gift of discernment enables a person to see into multiple layers of the heavens. The second and third heavens open up to someone with the gift of discernment. The first heaven is the atmosphere where we dwell on earth. The second heaven is the space over the earth that holds our solar system, sun, moon and stars. Lastly, the Throne of God sits in the third heaven. The Word reveals it here in Hebrews referencing more than one.

> **Heb. 4:14 (ASV)**
> *Seeing then that we have a great high priest, who has passed through the <u>heavens,</u> Jesus the Son of God, let us hold fast our profession.*

The first heaven is where we receive weather patterns, it is the firmament; the space we breathe, the air.

> **Gen 6:7 (ASV)**
> *And Jehovah said, I will destroy man whom I have created from the face of the ground; both man, and beast, and creeping things, and birds of the heavens; for it repenteth me that I have made them.*
>
> **James 5:18 (ASV)**
> *And he prayed again; and the heaven gave rain, and the earth brought forth her fruit.*

The solar system, outer space, exists in the second heaven. This is where the angelic and demonic beings communicate with us.

> **Mat 24:29 (ASV)**
> *But immediately after the tribulation of those days the sun shall be darkened, and the moon shall not give her light, and the stars shall fall from heaven, and the powers of the heavens shall be shaken.*
>
> **Deut. 4:19 (ASV)**
> *and lest thou lift up thine eyes unto heaven, and when thou seest the sun and the moon and the stars, even all the host of heaven, thou be drawn away and worship them, and serve them, which Jehovah thy God hath allotted unto all the peoples under the whole heaven.*

The third heaven is where the Throne of God rests. This is where our heavenly mansions are being prepared for us. This is the eternal, invisible realm. Jesus, the Lord of Hosts, and the Almighty God dwell here.

> **Deut. 10:14 (ASV)**
> *Indeed heaven and the highest heaves belong to the Lord your God, also the earth with all that is in it.*

***Psalm 148:4 (ASV)***
*Praise Him, you heaven of heavens
and you waters above the heavens!*

***1 Kings 8:27 (ASV)***
*But will indeed God dwell on the earth? Behold, heaven
and the heaven of heavens cannot contain you.*

The home of Father God, the Heaven of Heavens; His boundaries reflect there are no limitations for Him.

***Heb. 8:1 (ASV)***
*The point of what we are saying is this: We do have such
a high priest, who sat down at the right hand of the
Majesty in heaven.*

My whole Christian life I have operated in these three realms. Within a few months of asking Jesus to come live in my heart, I began to experience all three realms. After about six months in the Lord, I became very depressed. I would mope around the house in such lethargy, feeling manically depressed. However, when I would leave the house, visit people, go shopping, and such, I would be my bubbly self. Upon returning back to the apartment, I would find myself so oppressed and down again, hardly functioning. One day my spiritual mother said, "Cheryl, I have a word of knowledge for you." (The Bible calls that a supernatural word from God that you didn't know about a situation.) She had been a Christian her entire life and was responding sheepishly, hesitant to even give what she had received. She stated, "I keep getting the word 'pornography'. You don't have any pornography do you?" I said, with gusto, "Of course! Doesn't everyone?". She was a good Christian woman, raised in a Christian home. I was a baby Christian who only knew worldly, heathen ways. I only had a year of Catholic Church upbringing in my growing up years.

By this point, I had been dealing with this depression for almost six months. Wayne and I had been married six months and we were newlyweds. Wayne had noticed the severity of my depression and said, "What can I do for you? I'll do anything to make you better." So after receiving the word of knowledge about pornography that night, around midnight, I left my spiritual mother's house and went home to wake him up. I told him what my spiritual mom had shared with me. "Cheryl, you can't have pornography in your home. That is an open door for Satan to live in your home. You have to get rid of that. That is what is making you depressed." Well, my husband said, "Ok, I'll remove it in the morning." I said, "No! You have to do it right now because of what I am seeing in the spirit realm!"

That night was the night that the gift of discernment was activated in me by the Lord. It was as if a window shade went up on the inside of me and, all of a sudden, I was seeing into the spirit realm for the first time as a Christian. I had seen into the dark side as a child but I was re-awakened that day. I could see demons of all shapes and sizes that night. I saw demonic creatures and animals of all sorts around the apartment complex, so I left Wayne and he went back to bed. I quickly ran back to my spiritual mother's home to spend the night with her protection and she said, "You have to face this. You can't run". She wouldn't let me spend the night inside her home. I didn't exactly face it that night. Instead, I spent the night outside her house in the car talking with a friend.

The next day I decided to face it and went home. Wayne shared that, after I left, he had a terrible headache and felt a creepy presence in the room. He had not yet gone to church with me and had only come to the fun nights of our small group meetings. He shared over breakfast the next day that he just did what he had seen me do over the past nine months. He said, "I just cast it out in the name of Jesus!"

"REALLY?" I said, "You can't do that, you don't even know Jesus!" I asked, "Do you think maybe you ought to get to know this Jesus if you are using His name?" He said, "Yes". I called my spiritual mom and said, "Wayne is ready, I am bringing him over now. I don't know what to do with him".

I went into the back of her house, praying with fear and trembling, while Wayne and her were in the front room reading and praying as she began to walk him through the Romans Road of Salvation.* She read scriptures and certain passages that explained what the Bible says as to why, who, and what we need a Savior for. He asked Jesus into His heart that day.

It was that night that I began seeing into the second heaven. I began seeing spirit beings and have ever since. I have encountered angels, demons, fallen angels, warrior angels, messenger angels and many other creatures that we don't have here on earth but that are in the other realms of the Kingdom, as recorded in Ezekiel 1:18.

Night after night, month after month, year after year I was being tormented by Satan as I slept. Every evil thing that you can think of happened at night in my dreams. Night after night seemed like forever. I didn't know, at the time, that my family bloodlines and background were full of witchcraft, horror, perversions, lust and murder. I didn't understand why I was being so tormented by the enemy now that I was saved. After about three years, I began crying out to God asking that, since I could see the evil side, would He please let me see the heavenly side with angels and heavenly experiences. "Lord, I want to see the godly manifestations of Your Kingdom, not just the demonic creatures and evil encounters." I then began encountering both godly angels and encounters from heaven, as well as the evil side.

However, it was a total of seven years that I was tormented daily. I had such a keen gift of discernment that even that first year I was saved I would pray for people and they would get delivered of demons, by the grace of God. Many people I ministered to over the seven years would get totally set free from the demons they had been carrying all their lives. Then I would go home and those same demons would jump on me and torment me all night, sometimes for days and weeks. We would go on spiritual prayer drives and cast out the enemy in certain places geographically and the demons would come home and torment me; I would be in physical and mental pain crying out scriptures I knew, and prayers, all night long as the demons would beat me up.

Over and over Wayne would pray with me when I would wake him during one of my tormenting dreams. I didn't know how to stop it. After I got saved, I personally sought deliverance (the expulsion of demons from the soul) week after week, and each week I would get set free of different issues. Each Sunday I would go ask for prayer to be free from the tormenting spirits that were on the inside of me. I would also minister every week. I would minister and pray off demons that were "on" and "in" others. I was moving in God's power and discernment even though I was full of demonic strongholds and demons myself.

While all this was happening, I was growing by leaps and bounds in the Kingdom. I was a sponge. I ate, drank, and slept practically everything my spiritual mother and her six friends fed me every week. They would get together just to play cards and after a few hands, the power of God in them would make the demons in me start to tremble, shake and manifest in their presence. Each evening would end with them casting demons out of me. This happened week after week for several years. **Our past can affect our future until it is fully surrendered, repented of, and placed under the blood.** That's why we can be saved and still be affected by cycles of wrong behaviors, triggers from traumas, unforgiveness toward others, generational curses and strongholds.

Growing up, my parents would sit me in front of the TV at night with scary movies like Frankenstein, Mummy, Dracula, Werewolves, etc. This happened to me early on, from a toddler up, and I would have encounters from demons as a child with them manifesting as monsters in my room at night. Other demonic creatures would visit me at night as well. When I got saved and began trusting Jesus as my Savior, He began healing me of those demonic encounters.

One afternoon while sitting on a friend's couch, she discerned I had had some alcohol on my vacation a few days prior to our meeting. She mentioned it to me and shared her beliefs that Christians shouldn't drink. I didn't give it much thought and as we started to pray together, the Lord spoke to me personally and said, "I don't want alcohol to ever touch your lips. Don't ever drink alcohol again." So I repented for drinking. A little background -- my father and his father, and my mother's father, were all alcoholics. I grew up with two children of adult alcoholics (ACOA) and my dad had become one. This was a generational curse (something harmful passed through the generations due to iniquitous sin patterns) the Lord wanted me delivered of.

As soon as I repented, I had a vision. I saw a dark stage and on the stage were all those childhood monsters in a dreadful setting. They were all moving about like they were in charge and trying to scare me. Then all of a sudden, I saw the Blood of Jesus start at the top of the stage and begin to pour down over the entire scene. Drops of blood were melting the monsters right before my eyes! (Just like with the witch in the Wizard of Oz.) Then I saw a bright light and three dancing swords came into the room, with bright golden handles and silver reflective blades. They were dancing all over the room and in my soul that once held monsters in it. Discernment empowered me to receive deliverance from the demons of torment and from the monsters in my nightmares. This was the first vision the Holy Spirit used to begin to bring healing to my wounded, demonized soul.

In addition to discernment, my other gifts were growing as well. My ability to hear the Lord in words of wisdom, healing, prophecy, and sharing Jesus' love were coming forth. I would minister to everyone around me by praying, sharing visions and prophetic words I received. The power of God moved through me and I desired even more to pursue the Kingdom and God's gift of discernment.

One day the Lord spoke to me to have a baby (previous chapter) and I struggled with that word. I needed to have extra prayer to enable me to move forward on that word. I set up an appointment with a small ministry team (SMT) at church to pray with me for six weeks over my past abortion experience, coupled with my dysfunctional parental experiences. Having both issues in my background did not lend itself to my being emotionally ready to have a child.

I had been saved seven years at this point, and as I met for six weeks with this SMT consisting of my Pastor and another Pastor's wife, they began to share with me that I had a "false gift of discernment". I was livid! "IMPOSSIBLE!" I said, "For seven years I have prayed for people, houses and locations in the city and demons flee every time! Many people have received deliverance from my praying with them. How can that be a false gift of discernment?" It took a few weeks to soak in, but after seven years of torment day in and day out, I wanted FREE! I finally agreed to listen to them and, sure enough, due to my family history of witchcraft, Satan wanted to stop me from moving forward in the Kingdom. The Lord revealed to me that every time I operated in discerning of spirits and cast them out, it was the enemy revealing the enemy's presence there. That had kept a family generational door open for Satan's demons to turn around and torment me. It was like having a target on your back saying, "Here I am! Come shoot me!" (Acts 19:11-20). I understand what it means to be beat up and overpowered by demonic forces. I so appreciate that day of deliverance and the true discernment of those two women who stood up to me! I was finally free after seven years! GOD set me free from those familiar spirits of my family and my true gift of discernment was no longer hindered by demonic interference.

From that day forward I could pray for someone, a home or the city, and not have demons come after me and retaliate! I began sleeping without nightmares and began hearing and seeing angels more and more. The Holy Spirit began increasing His interactions with me. I began having godly dreams. I praise God for that day of deliverance! Thank you, Pam and Tina, for your service of time and love. The promise of God came forth, even though sometimes we have to wait for the manifestation of His Word. His promises are true. Isaiah 55:11 paraphrased says, that His Word will accomplish what it is sent to do and will not come back void.

Over the years Satan has tried to scare me, kill me, and stop me from moving forward into my designed purpose and call. He overplays his hand and has exposed me to many various issues of the satanic realms and hierarchies. Jesus has used me to serve others in being set free in these areas. In addition, the Lord has gifted and empowered me with His deep abiding love to tear down strongholds in regions, cities, churches and individuals. He has sent me around the globe to: Belarus, Israel, Virgin Islands, and countless cities and states in America bringing discernment and deliverance to many. In 1 John 3:8 it states that Jesus came to destroy the works of the enemy. We are partners in that plan and promise! Whatever the enemy has ensnared you with, God can set you free and the Lord will use you to set others free! Your inheritance in the Kingdom of God is the liberty and freedom you have in Christ (John 8:36). We are liberated so that we can be liberators through Christ. You can walk in this gift and set the captives free. Who do you know that needs freedom, bound in chains they can't be free of? You can take the scriptures and share them. You can take your story and share it so that others can be set free by what Jesus has set you free from. This is the promise of God for you in Isaiah 61.

### *Isaiah 61 Living Bible (TLB)*

*61 The Spirit of the Lord God is upon me, because the Lord has anointed me to bring good news to the suffering and afflicted. He has sent me to comfort the brokenhearted, to announce liberty to captives, and to open the eyes of the blind. 2 He has sent me to tell those who mourn that the time of God's favor to them has come, and the day of his wrath to their enemies. 3 To all who mourn in Israel he will give: beauty for ashes; joy instead of mourning; praise instead of heaviness. For God has planted them like strong and graceful oaks for his own glory. 4 And they shall rebuild the ancient ruins, repairing cities long ago destroyed, reviving them though they have lain there many generations.*
*5 Foreigners shall be your servants; they shall feed your flocks and plow your fields and tend your vineyards.*
*6 You shall be called priests of the Lord, ministers of our God. You shall be fed with the treasures of the nations and shall glory in their riches. 7 Instead of shame and dishonor, you shall have a double portion of prosperity and everlasting joy. 8 For I, the Lord, love justice; I hate robbery and wrong. I will faithfully reward my people for their suffering and make an everlasting covenant with them. 9 Their descendants shall be known and honored among the nations; all shall realize that they are a people God has blessed. 10 Let me tell you how happy God has made me! For he has clothed me with*

*garments of salvation and draped about me the robe of righteousness. I am like a bridegroom in his wedding suit or a bride with her jewels. 11 The Lord will show the nations of the world his justice; all will praise him His righteousness shall be like a budding tree, or like a garden in early spring, full of young plants springing up everywhere. Praise the Lord!*

Note:

*In the Resources is a link to the <u>Romans Road of Salvation</u>, scriptures for prayer. To receive freedom from demonic oppression or possession one must first authentically want Jesus to be the Lord of your life. Go back to chapter 1 and pray the prayer point to receive Jesus as your Lord and Savior.

Have you suffered under the effects of demonic torment or know someone who has? There is resource material in the back of this book on how to pray through this model of deliverance "<u>Footsteps to Freedom</u>".[1]

*Please note! This is not an activity to be done alone. It is advised that you find a Pastor, a leader in your church or small group to pray these prayers together. Where two or more are gathered, He is in our midst. When we confess our sins one to another, we shall be healed. Two can put 10,000 demons to flight. There is more power and authority in agreement. If you are not willing to give up your behavior and you receive deliverance you will have 7 times more affliction and torment then you did before you received deliverance. You must be completely sure you no longer want this in your life. It is also advised to consider fasting before praying for deliverance.*

**Prayer Point**

(I recommend worship music playing during times of prayer. Also, you will need to repeat this process for each issue or demonic oppression you're facing.)

Dear Lord Jesus,

1. I *acknowledge* Your blood that was shed on Calvary for the cleansing of my sins and deliverance. There is power in the BLOOD and the Name of JESUS.

2. I *surrender* all guards and guardians over my heart to You, Jesus. I trust You.

3. I forgive _____ (name) for _____ (action/hurt). I forgive myself for my sin and/sin responses of _____.

4. I *invoke* the power of the Blood and the Name of Jesus over all demonic powers that are tormenting me.

5. I *repent* for the sin of _____.

6. I *renounce* the activities/actions of _____ that accompanied my sin.

7. I *step out of agreement* with this sin and its behaviors now, in Jesus' name.

8. I *declare* there shall be no discomforting manifestations by any demons in Jesus' name, just obedience to the Blood and Name of Jesus.

9. I *rebuke* the demon(s) of _____ & renounce them. Leave my soul, in Jesus' name.

10. I *choose* Jesus to be Lord over this area of _____ in my life.

11. I *submit* my will and actions to be obedient to Jesus and the Comforter (Holy Spirit), by His grace.

12. I *receive* the Holy Spirit to aid me with His power, to overcome and fill this empty space with Himself now, in Jesus' name.

13. I *commit* to maintaining my deliverance through reading the Word, worshipping and being accountable to my leaders/church family.

14. I *seal* my deliverance in the Blood of the Lamb and the power of His Spirit by the authority given to me in His Word. (Is 61:1, John 6:27, 8:36, 10:10, 10:17, Luke 4 1-14, 8:26-39, 10:19, Mk 5:1-20, 2 Cor. 1:21-22, Eph. 1:13-14)

CHERYL CLINTON WEAVER

## *THE KING, THE CROSS AND ME*

Who is this King of grace and glory
This Son of Man, this Jesus from Galilee
Who seems so much like you and me
This Jesus who is born of the heavenly Father
The God of truth and purity
For this day, the Son of Man was born
Born into a manger
Proclaimed a king, of Him the angels did sing
He is Jesus, our Lord and King
A Son to glorify his Father
The God of everything
For this Kingdom He was formed
This Kingdom that stretches across eternity

Now this King hangs on Calvary
His crime is simple
Too much love for humanity
Jesus who knew his Father's will
Submitted his all in humility
He lay himself upon that Cross
To make his covenant complete
Pouring out his life's blood
Not in defeat, but victory!
The sign they hung above his head
Proclaimed his Kingdom to all who see
This man Jesus, the Messiah
Is our Lord and Majesty

Now I stand in complete liberty
Bought, paid for, blessed and set free!
Your salvation of me, a precious gift
Given by the blood You shed on Calvary
Lord, I am healed and made whole
By the stripes You bore for me
Jesus You are my heart, my love, my goodness
Your grace and peace abound in me
Lord, Your love and mercy go hand in hand
You are the Rock on which I stand
Jesus, Your love goes ahead of me
To prepare a place (where I will be) in heaven
Where I will dwell for eternity!

*Betty Clinton*
*April 12, 1999*

## CHAPTER SIX
# THE PROMISE OF HIS WORD

His Healing Word Exonerates Accusation

Have you ever had someone accuse you of something that you didn't do? Have you ever accused someone of doing something and then found them to be innocent? This is what happened to our Savior, Jesus Christ. He was accused, berated, beaten, skin ripped, and crucified on a cross to set all humanity free from sin and death. He was crucified by the Romans as demanded by the Jewish (religious people) leaders of the time. They feared him even though he was an innocent man! All of this was allowed by the heavenly Father.

Many of us have experienced being accused of something; some things we were guilty of and some we were not. A simple misgiving from time to time can be forgiven. As humility is present, we choose to overlook and love instead of react in our own sin response patterns.

However, what happens when that accusation is repetitive and/or unrepentant? What action is taken when there is a constant action that is repeated over and over? I believe situations such as this can be induced by a spiritual force; a force that is returning to bring us as believers down, preventing us from reaping the fullness of relationship we can have as His children!

The Bible says that Satan is the accuser of the brethren. As children of the Promise we all have to deal with the accusations that come from the enemy of our soul. However, **God's Word is the promise that defeats the accusation.**

*Revelation 12:10-11 (KJV)*
*[10] And I heard a loud voice saying in heaven, Now is come salvation, and strength, and the kingdom of our God, and the power of his Christ: for the accuser of our brethren is cast down, which accused them before our God day and night. [11]* ***And they overcame him by the blood of the Lamb, and by the word of their testimony; and they loved not their lives unto the death.***

*Isaiah 54:17 (KJV)*
*[17] No weapon that is formed against thee shall prosper; and every tongue that shall rise against thee in judgment* ***thou shalt condemn****. This is the heritage of the servants of the LORD, and their righteousness is of me, saith the LORD.*

*Romans 8:1-2 (KJV)*
*[1] There is therefore* ***now no condemnation to them*** *which are in Christ Jesus, who walk not after the flesh, but after the Spirit. [2] For the law of the Spirit of life in Christ Jesus hath made me free from the law of sin and death.*

I lived with the spirit of accusation in my life for many, many years – actually, from birth. It would manifest on a daily basis as a critical spirit, a constant negative word against me, or a blame shifting from others who would take no responsibility for their own sin. I was influenced to be accusing of others and myself constantly in my self-talk and in my real moments when life would get hard.

But GOD! I can't say that enough! BUT GOD! He is my Deliverer! **He is your Deliverer!** He is alive and He desires to set us free from the sins that so easily entangle us. King David says, "Search my heart, oh God!" This is the cry of my heart as well! As I was seeking the Lord about why I couldn't get breakthrough, He gave me a dream about the "spirit of accusation".

I pressed in, asking about accusation and where did it come from, and I remembered a woman on my front lawn a few months prior accusing me of things that I did not do. She was falsely accusing me. I knew that was the open door for the recent increase of accusations around me and in my mind. So I asked, "Ok, why was that allowed to stay and why has this been a pattern in my life, Lord?" I was resting in my quiet time with the Lord and the Holy Spirit took me back to when I was conceived in my mother's womb out of wedlock.* The Holy Spirit showed me three things: 1) My father did not want to have children at that time so he made accusations, and I received them in the womb. Those accusations were seeded into my spiritual DNA; 2) My father did not take responsibility that he contributed to the situation of making a child; and, 3) Blame shifting became seeded into me spiritually.

The Holy Spirit then took me to when I was about five years old, and I was very close to my Daddy (the minute I was born he adored me and we spent all our time together). I went to work with him every day, I was his little princess and we shared our time together all over town – we even ate the same foods at the same time! Then, circumstances changed dramatically. He had to start working in a factory to provide for my new baby brother and me; I started school and we moved. Life from that time forward for me was drastically different. My father became distant and unavailable, both emotionally and physically. I experienced a great loss! However, as a five year old, I didn't know how to process that loss and equated loss with my own failure. Somehow, I felt that I had failed and caused all the breakdown of his love and adoration. I agreed with the lie, "I am a failure". That label was part of the foundational structure upon which my entire adulthood was created.

Thank God we have a heavenly Father that loves and cherishes us. No one can ever take that away! The Lord showed me that I had built a pyramid of false structures and coping mechanisms to cover over or replace the void and loss of relational love that only a father can provide. As I began to forgive him for his responses and forgive the circumstances, the Lord began to uncover the false structures.

First, there were the accusations of the neighbor lady and my dad. That was all I knew about and all I thought I was dealing with. Then, the Spirit revealed that in my soul under the accusations, was a deep pocket of disappointment. I began to release the groans and cries of disappointments that I had carried in my soul with my dad. I was touched by the Spirit to go deeper and under the disappointments I came face-to-face with great grief and loss.

However, I shifted immediately into a sense of failure. "Why am I feeling failure?" I asked myself. Instead of dealing with the experience of "grief and loss", being unable to process that as a five year old, I took my father's sin upon myself. I agreed with the lie of Satan that "I was a failure". This became my belief and dictated how I saw myself. I escaped the grief and loss (so my psyche thought) burying it down deep and moved to a works mentality, striving to do everything in life to overwrite that subconscious label on my forehead. Have you ever struggled with your soul like this?

Abba Father is our great Deliverer toward healing and wholeness! I forgave my father and I repented for not trusting God and using failure as an escape route that ensnared me into an unending cycle of self-accusations. I released the grief and sorrow of the loss that the little girl inside of me needed freedom from. Then, I saw that I had legalistically built self-imposed structures to live by, thus providing myself a false sense of acceptance. I did this due to my own self-coping to overcome the label of "failure". When

I surrendered to God and renounced (fell out of agreement with) the lie, Jesus came and tore down the pyramid of self-created, self-understanding structures. Now before all that happened, if you would have asked me, "Did you feel like a failure?" I would have said, "No way!". However, God sees all and He sees into the heart of all men. Nothing is hidden from God.

God's Word says quite the contrary about who we are and who He is in us. We are not a failure. We are His Beloved, His Saints and a Royal Priesthood. I have a new level of freedom and peace that only Jesus can give by the blood He shed on the Cross. Jesus took all my grief, sorrow, fear, failure, shame and accusations onto the Cross with Him; an innocent man who loved me so much He BORE MY SINS and the SINS of my father to give me the liberty to walk healed and whole in Him. It is a divine exchange -- the great mystery of the Gospel. He that was without sin became sin for us!

How I shout for JOY at the One who loves us so much that He cares about what we care about! There is no other Name above all the earth and there is no other God that personally touches the deepest parts of our soul with His healing love removing every wound and scar, replacing them with grace and peace. When we serve Christ and lay down our lives, we learn to enter into the sufferings of Christ Jesus as He suffered for us. We will also suffer for the joy that is set before us -- Christ the King! (1 Pet. 2:21, 4:13, Heb. 12:2)

> *Matthew 27:37 (KJV)*
> *37 And set up over his head his accusation written, THIS IS JESUS THE KING OF THE JEWS.*

**However, there was and is not any accusation that held Jesus down, or that can hold us down!** Yes, as we become more and more like Christ (this is an aspect of our walk), we will overcome. Jesus has given us His promise that His taking our accusation on the Cross covers every other accusation that could ever be spewed at us. Hallelujah!

*See Resources Section – How to break the bastard curse.*

## PRAYER POINT (Repeat out loud)

> I repent first for any and every accusation that I have made against (names) _____. I choose to forgive them.
> Any accusations that I have made against you God, Jesus or the Holy Spirit, I repent for my sin and ask for Your forgiveness. I forgive myself.
> In any place where the Accuser has come against me, I surrender it to the Cross and into the depths of your love Father, through the Blood of Jesus. I repent of my sin responses.
> I repent of any judgments against others that I have made (list them and who, if you know). I break the harvest of those judgments now against myself and my children. I thank you Jesus that you are using this to grow me into your image. I forgive and bless those who curse me.
> I release my Father's warrior angels to go forth now and repudiate, restore and bring righteous judgment with restitution and healing to my soul, in Jesus' name. The Word of God is like a hammer that smashes the rock and I declare that all accusations against me be smashed, cease and desist now in Jesus' name. Every tongue that rises up against me shall be refuted. Isaiah 54:16-17. Amen!

## ***THE SPIRIT***

Love,
Mercy
Grace
Joy
Peace
Patience
Humility
Goodness
Gentleness
Faithfulness
Self-control
Forgiveness
Kindness
Purity
Unity
Fill your vessel with the blessings of Jesus
Then pour out your anointing on others
His miracle will work through you
For the glory of the Father. Amen.

*Betty Clinton*
*August 26, 1999*

## CHAPTER SEVEN
# THE PROMISE OF PEACE

Compromise Resists the Promise of Peace

At 25 years of age, I was ready for a fresh start in life. Wayne Weaver (my boyfriend of five years) had agreed that I should move from Indiana to Florida to be closer to my family. I was shocked that he came over to help me pack & see me off because I had secretly hoped he would propose instead. After three months of being in Florida (and both of us single), he came to visit. As we were sitting on a sunset beach in Clearwater, Florida, he proposed. We had dated off and on over the five years I had known him and I immediately said, "YES!" The following week we rented the dress and the tux, purchased the rings, registered the license at the courthouse, and the following Sunday we chartered a 45-foot sailboat in the Gulf of Mexico and were married! I have lots of family in the area, so one opened her home, another bought a cake, and another purchased flowers and, "voilà!" a reception within a week. My family is gifted in putting on a party!

It was amazing, except for one little thing -- my wedding ring. It was a "compromise". I had been previously engaged to another man before my husband proposed. We had broken up some time before Wayne. However, I kept the diamond ring from that engagement. I loved the marque design, so to save money and provide me with a ring I really liked, I suggested taking the marque out of the old engagement ring and placing it in the new wedding set. BIG MISTAKE! Did I say mistake?

Well, that was an understatement! I wasn't saved at the time and I really didn't see any problem with doing that.

Wayne and I DID, however, receive Jesus the following year after our wedding. Over the next seven years I had horrible, tormenting sexual dreams night after night involving my ex-fiancé. I did not know I had a soul-tie with my ex-fiancé. (A soul-tie is commonly known as a sexual tie that creates a bondage in your soul tying you to another person whom you have been physically intimate with. Soul-ties must be broken by repentance from fornication and applying the Blood of Jesus. Paul, in scripture, states that sexual sin is the only sin that affects the soul because the two shall become one flesh and we leave fragments of ourselves with the other person.)

The Lord was trying to speak to me about the ring, but I was not hearing. The first time I realized the Lord was telling me that I had to get rid of the $4,000.00 marquee I thought, "Devil, get thee behind me!". It is funny now to look back on. My pride and my compromise were robbing me in my relationship with my husband. Compromise came at a high cost for me in our intimacy as a couple, my sleep, and my relationship with the Lord.

We use rings as a symbol of our marriage covenant agreement between God and man and woman. I was virtually married to two people, in the spiritual sense. After prophetic and scriptural confirmations, and much prayer, my husband and I agreed to let go of the marquee diamond. The Lord was gracious! We found a jeweler who took it in on a trade. We had received a bonus that month and were able to get a beautiful .75 caret round diamond for our eighth anniversary (prophetically eight means new beginnings). We dedicated it to God and our marriage. A new beginning! Everything shifted in our marriage and in my walk with the Lord. God asked us to have a baby right after that! (I shared this in a previous chapter.)

No one wakes up one morning and says, "I am going to compromise, lower my integrity, and become a man or woman of ill repute.". This is a slow, degrading process which is like the proverbial frog in the pot of boiling water that doesn't realize it's being cooked. We end up in a situation that is uncomfortable, but somehow the voices speak to us. We continue to acquiesce and relinquish what we know is right for some ulterior benefit that satiates us, yet it's temporarily drowning out our current consciousness causing numbness, guilt, or worse -- a stony heart that just doesn't care anymore. The dictionary describes compromise as, "a mutual dispute settled by concession".

In the world today it is imperative that we can see and know when something is of God and something is not of God. The best way I have learned to discern is by asking this question out loud whenever it was unclear who I was hearing from. The enemy always has to answer this question. "Do you believe Jesus Christ is the Son of God, who was born of the Virgin Mary, died on the Cross and was resurrected?" Then wait for your answer!

> ***1 John 4:1-3 (ASV)***
> *¹ Beloved, believe not every spirit, but prove the spirits, whether they are of God; because many false prophets are gone out into the world. ² Hereby know ye the Spirit of God: every spirit that confesseth that Jesus Christ is come in the flesh is of God: ³ and every spirit that*

*confesseth not Jesus is not of God: and this is the spirit of the antichrist, whereof ye have heard that it cometh; and now it is in the world already.*

Learning discernment from the Holy Spirit is part of defining our maturity in Jesus. In my early 20's I had a saying that I used a lot as a young professional, "Concessions without conditions equals no value.". If we understand that there was a high price paid for the freedom we now explore on a daily basis as blood-bought believers, we wouldn't trample the Gospel underfoot with compromise. The Gospel is a free gift to anyone who will choose to believe on Jesus and make Him their Lord. However, it is a costly gift and has great value even though, for you and I, we can receive this as a true gift for which someone else has paid. PRICELESS!

When you COMPROMISE you receive a decrease in value. When you decrease your value, it affects your soul; you lose integrity. When you lose integrity, you weaken your character. When your character is weakened, you lose your witness. A weakened character creates a loss of WITNESS. **Thus, compromising the Truth weakens your WITNESS and IDENTITY.** If you have weakened your identity, then your witness is not credible. Then we begin to be someone who isn't walking out the Gospel and that's when non-believers start to call us hypocrites.

We cannot, nor do we have a right to, try and compromise with God. God is TRUTH, RIGHTEOUSNESS, and HOLINESS. He cannot compromise His Word or His plumbline standards for anyone.

> ***Isaiah 28:17-18 (NLT)***
> *I will take the measuring line of justice and the plumb line of righteousness to check the foundation wall you have built. Your refuge looks strong, but since it is made of lies, a hailstorm will knock it down. Since it is made of*

> *deception the enemy will come like a flood to sweep it away. I will cancel the bargain you made to avoid death, and I will overturn your deal to dodge the grave.*

When we attempt to compromise in the Kingdom we are placing God at our level and demanding that He become what we want Him to be vs. WHO HE REALLY IS. We can't make God in our image. HE IS GOD. We start and finish at His Holy plumbline, not at our limited standard and knowledge.

The Gospel can't be compromised. Man can try to concede man's will and man's ways and project that on our Lord, but it will always fail because God does not change, as His Word says. If you are trying to measure yourself with your standard against His, you will always come up short. This is a tactic of the enemy and the flesh to get us to measure up through our own eyes, abilities and ways. We have to start with the blood and receive the full righteousness He has already established as His perfect plumbline. We have to start with what Jesus has done and not what we have done. To face that is to let go of our compromised state of rationalization for our behaviors and sins and fully surrender to what Jesus died for. It is only when we come to the end of ourselves, and the end of compromise, that we can truly receive the fullness of God's promises.

> **2 Cor. 10:5**
> **Putting an end to <u>reasoning's</u>, and every high thing which is lifted up against the knowledge of God, and causing every thought to come under the authority of Christ;** [6] *Being ready to give punishment to whatever is against his authority, after you have made it clear that you are completely under his control.*

Money, diamonds and power -- none of these are worth compromising my wonderful relationship of peace with my heavenly Father. Choosing Jesus' will over mine and His righteousness provided me freedom from demonic sexual night terrors and helped close one of the open doors to generational curses of adultery in my husband's and my own bloodlines. This was interfering with our personal intimacy as man and wife. We are now able to enter into a deeper level of wholeness, fullness, intimacy and promise from the Father regarding our marriage.

**Prayer Point**

Lord, I repent, renounce, and let go of all compromise, half-heartedness and lukewarmness in my soul. I choose to fully engage You, look You straight in the eyes with true confession in my soul, holding nothing back. I repent where my compromises have hurt other people. (The Lord may ask you over time to personally repent to them face-to-face, as He leads.) I choose to forgive others whose compromises have affected me. I choose to forgive myself where I have compromised. I ask You, Lord, for Your fullness of peace that passes my understanding in Jesus' name. Help me, Jesus, to walk in integrity and by your grace uphold your Word. Amen.

## *The Word Became Flesh I*

WORDS
The words of a pen, mouth, book, a person
Words can encourage, educate,
and make people laugh or cry
The spoken word can escalate, evaluate a person's worth
Open a heart or close a door
Words can diminish or uplift
Words give power and life or death and destruction

WORDS
Simple, overlooked, time, details
In the large grand scheme of life, a day, an hour
No one ever thinks about or focuses on simple words
Except One Person, a very incredible Being who speaks
Truth
In riddles and parables in darkness –
releases life in syllables
One Being – three parts
One Book - Eternal Life

Cheryl Weaver
July 2009

UNBROKEN PROMISES

## CHAPTER EIGHT
# THE PROMISE OF FORGIVENESS

Dealing with our sin responses betrayal, rejection, abandonment, anger, abuse, lies, and deception are all a myriad of sins that weigh us down. Hurting people always hurt people. Many of us walk around with huge suitcases of unforgiveness. Why do I say suitcases? Well you see, unforgiveness is never the only issue at hand; it is always connected to something else like hurt, abuse or injustice. Hence, our suitcases are full of trauma; our soul is carrying extra baggage.

This subject is not a popular one when the time comes that we need to forgive others. However, unforgiveness is the lock that keeps all the HURT buried deep inside our heart and soul. Our mind pretends to cover up all the pain with justification, but unfortunately, it still remains locked in our suitcase of trauma. **The key to releasing the hurt and unlocking the buried baggage is to forgive!**

**The process towards any healing is the ability to forgive.** Many think forgiveness is a "feeling" and we must "FEEL" like forgiving to ascertain the ability. Nothing could be further from the truth. Forgiveness is an act of our will; it's a choice. Our "will" manages our emotions (at least it should). For instance, if someone offered you one million dollars to refrain from anger for 30 days, would you choose not to allow your emotions to override your will so you could receive your million-dollar reward? We often don't lack ability, just motivation. Forgiveness is not any different. Yes, we have been wounded, offended and betrayed, but forgiveness is the only key that will unlock our hearts and let us out of the bondage of hurt that is holding us captive. It's time to release the suitcases!

We are made up of three parts: mind, body and soul. Our body is subject to our mind. Our soul is subject to our spiritual choices -- our choice of Christ or Satan. Any lack of choice on our part always defaults to Satan being in control over us, for he is the god of this world. The will, our mind, chooses daily our options and directions to move in. We have the ability to choose! This is one of the free gifts that Creator-God gave to His creation; the ability to choose who you want to serve. In this time of making choices we can choose to rule over our emotions and feelings. It is a good thing to "command" your emotions and feelings to be under the Word of God and submitted to Christ and not allow the flesh to rule over your will. Second Corinthians states it like this:

> ***2 Corinthians 10:1-16 (BBE)***
> *[1] Now I, Paul, myself make request to you by the quiet and gentle behaviour of Christ, I who am poor in spirit when with you, but who say what is in my mind to you without fear when I am away from you: [2] Yes, I make my request to you, so that when I am with you I may not have to make use of the authority which may be needed against some to whom seem to be walking after the flesh. [3] For though we may be living in the flesh, we are not fighting after the way of the flesh [4] (For the arms with which we are fighting are not those of the flesh, but are strong before God for the destruction of high places); [5] Putting an end to reasonings, and every high thing which is lifted up against the knowledge of God, and causing every thought to come under the authority of Christ; [6] Being ready to give punishment to whatever is against his authority, after you have made it clear that you are completely under his control.*

Once we pray along these lines, we see how much we are

governed by the flesh, feelings and emotions. Another test to see if you are being driven by emotions and reactions verses being driven by choices is to hold a time of fasting. Immediately, when you give up food, you learn quickly who is leading whom!

> ***Nehemiah 9:1-3 (King James Version)***
> *Now in the twenty and fourth day of this month the children of Israel were assembled with fasting, and with sack clothes, and earth upon them. And the seed of Israel separated themselves from all strangers, and stood and confessed their sins, and the iniquities of their fathers. And they stood up in their place, and read in the book of the law of the LORD their God one fourth part of the day; and another fourth part they confessed, and worshipped the LORD their God.*

The people in life that I have had to forgive the most have been my dad and my grandfather. When I am ministering, I often share with the person whom I am praying for that "God is the Daddy that we wished our daddies here on earth would have been, but weren't." Papa God is nothing like so many of our earthly fathers that seemed to fail us. You may have had a wonderful father, mother and family life, and your parents may have modeled life for you in a godly manner, supporting and propelling you into adulthood with their many blessings. If that is your story, I am grateful for you and the godly examples that Papa God has provided! However, there are countless numbers of us who have lived in dysfunctional homes. We had fathers and mothers that lacked the love and ability to give us what we needed. It is for these that I want to stand in proxy (as if I am one of them) and say to you – "<u>I am sorry!</u>" **After the Name and Blood of Jesus, the two most powerful words on the planet are "I'M SORRY".** (*[1] See the end of the chapter for a special prayer of repentance in proxy for you.)

Our response to Abba Father is to be like Jesus. His response to the multitudes that betrayed him and demanded that He be crucified on the Cross of Calvary was, "Father forgive them, for they know not what they do!" I can imagine your response to this regarding those that have hurt you -- *"They knew **exactly** what they were doing!"* However, I choose to give people the benefit of the doubt when it comes to love and compassion and trust. I tend to think, "If that person had different circumstances, more knowledge, wisdom and healing, perhaps they would have responded differently." We have an opportunity to respond with maturity and Christlikeness when someone sins against us. We have an opportunity for a divine exchange; to be like Jesus as His nature overtakes ours. He chose to pick up the Cross, the weight of our sin, and He is asking us to do the same. We are to choose to pick up our cross, and the weight of their sins against us, by forgiving them. We nail our pain (suitcase) to the Cross with Jesus because He already bore it all for us over 2,000 years ago.

Remember, we aren't looking to our feelings right now. We are walking in obedience to the Word of God. The Lord's Prayer states it like this:

> **Luke 11:4 (KJV)**
> [4] And forgive us our sins; for we also forgive every one that is indebted to us. And lead us not into temptation; but deliver us from evil.

And in the following:

> **Ephesians 4:32 (KJV)**
> [32] And be ye kind one to another, tenderhearted, forgiving one another, even as God for Christ's sake hath forgiven you.

> **1 John 1:9 (KJV)**
> [9] If we confess our sins, he is faithful and just to forgive us our sins, and to cleanse us from all unrighteousness.

***James 5:16 (KJV)***
*16 Confess your faults one to another, and pray one for another, that ye may be healed. The effectual fervent prayer of a righteous man availeth much.*

We can literally release to the Cross the pain we are feeling from others who have sinned against us. Jesus will lift it off of us as we truly forgive and give it to Him. **It is after our act of obedience to forgive, then the feelings will follow.** When we make the choice to be in alignment with Heaven (alignment means choosing holiness and righteousness as our guide), our feelings and emotions begin to come into alignment as well.

It is important to be aware of the residual knocking at the door from Satan to tempt you to take your suitcase back and carry it around again. Remember, do not let the thoughts and arguments return; continue to submit them to the Cross firmly (over and over), resisting the enemy until the thoughts disappear (James 4:7). Satan's demons test our resolve to see if we really believe what we have proclaimed. They are always looking for a crack to wiggle back in **upon our agreement**. Often I use a prophetic act to enhance my actions to assist me in keeping the door closed. For example, I lift up my hand and say, "Talk to the hand!" (a symbol of, 'I am not listening!').

My trust and my truths were broken at age five. What we experience, we evaluate. What we evaluate, we determine. What we determine creates our dictates (an order or principle that must be obeyed). Our dictates become what we believe and, more often than not, these beliefs are lies.

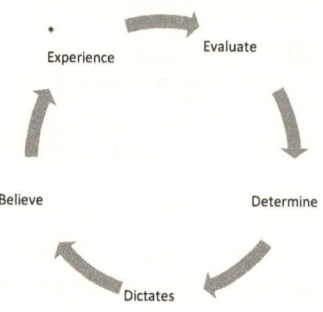

**Lies we agree with grow into strongholds in our soul.** Think of it this way -- a set of rose-colored glasses that we wear, filtering our perceptions until Jesus reveals the glasses are the lies we have agreed with.

I was a daddy's girl from the beginning. As a child I was gifted with charisma and my dad held me up on a pedestal and paraded me around as his little doll. Everything I was had to be perfect and perfectly in place to uphold this image he wanted to present (which dictated my life until I was 25). I did everything with my dad and just like my dad. We used to go to a restaurant called the Wagon Wheel and we would eat exactly the same thing. I always added ketchup because he added ketchup. I would go to work with my dad from age three to five. He managed a drive-in theater and I would help the cashiers hand out tickets. We would go to the post office together and the newspaper office. The employees adored me. I was always singing and charming them when I came in. My dad and I were two peas in a pod. I was his little princess and his showpiece to the world. Then one day in 1971 it all came crashing in like a freight train that had run off its rails. We moved, my dad started working in a factory, my brother was born (with three months of chronic colic) and I started school. Everything changed. I was no longer daddy's little girl. What little attention he had left after working all day in the factory was given to his new baby son. My mom was overwhelmed with a crying baby 24/7 and I was left to fend for myself amongst the cruelties of first graders.

My mom wanted to make sure I was taken care of and so she sent me to school with my dad's lunch box filled, and I mean filled to overflowing with food. (Because of her father's alcoholism her experience as a child was no food for her. This created the belief that to care for me she had to give me way more food than a 5 year old needed.) That is when I began to fill the void in my life with other things. I felt so abandoned. Once the center of my father's universe (in a dysfunctional way), I was now left with hurtful classmates. Did I have parents? Yes. Food? Yes. Basic needs met? Yes. However, that time of abandonment placed many lenses of delusion on me, and I agreed with every one of them. My experience led my 5 year old self to subconsciously evaluate it all. My evaluations determined decisions that became dictates creating beliefs that turned into strongholds for the rest of my life. They wrapped themselves around me like grave clothes to prevent me from moving into the true form of my identity and kept me from receiving Christ and bringing others to him. Negative dictates (lies) that we agree with entrench our soul like railroad tracks we have to follow.

But GOD! **The promise of forgiveness always brings healing. It's the fullness of the Gospel applied to the soul of man. It always produces fruit!** The railroad track (or stronghold – repeat cycles of behaviors that hold you in a pattern) that continued to repeat in every relationship in my life was, "I love you, but I can't spend time with you." Because of my internal dictates (an order or principle that we create like judgments and vows), *[2](See prayer at the end of the chapter.) I had the same pattern (stronghold) repeat itself over and over in all my relationships until I had an **encounter with the Lord**. That encounter overrode the first encounter (my dad's abandonment at five), exposed the lies, and opened the way of forgiveness -- I finally forgave him. I repented for my judgment and vows against him and myself, and Jesus cleansed it all in His blood. **The stronghold was broken; pain, abandonment and rejection were healed. His promise now fulfilled, praise the Lord!**

There can be generational strongholds as well. At the age of five my mother also experienced a far more grievous defilement. Her father (my grandfather) started molesting and raping her. The stronghold was a family pattern of destruction from the enemy to attack the children at the age of five. She was continuously abused, both sexually and physically, until she was 16 years old. Her trust and truth were extremely broken and violated. Heinous violations of parental trust gets reprogrammed and reinstalled in children's' psyches as "good is evil and evil is good" when continual abuse is present. My grandfather not only abused her but also shared her with his brother and, when he ran out of drinking money, sold her to the local boys for cash. Some of us can probably relate to this as one out of every five women have been sexually assaulted, and one out of every seventy men.*[3]

As my relationship with my mom grew over the years, I would find out more and more details about the severity of her abuse. But God! My mom literally died at the hands of her abuser at five years of age. She left her body and sat on the lap of Jesus. Jesus loved on her and offered her a choice. She could choose to stay in heaven or come back to earth. He explained that He had "an assignment for her on the earth: that her children and grandchildren would make a difference on the earth for Him." She decided to come back and suffered 11 more years of abuse. When she came of age she joined the Army to escape. She met my dad, married, and had me at the age of 19. Later in life, I had the privilege to lead both my mom and my dad to the Lord.

The Word says, *"For His thoughts are not our thoughts, as far as the heavens are higher than the earth, so are my ways higher than your ways, and my thoughts than your thoughts."* We on this side of heaven think, "How could a loving God allow this?" God sees the beginning and the end. We do not. He knows the good that will come from temporary suffering. We do not. We don't always get to see the benefits or the bigger picture. We have to trust that He is GOOD and He only has our best interests at heart -- that's faith! Remember, He gave us all a free will and not everyone chooses to do the right thing. Satan's dominion is the earth realm and he rules over the hearts of humanity that are not submitted to Jesus. Evil exists. It's ugly and destructive, it mars and stains, and it is maleficent. That is why God sent a Savior to save us!

My mom not only forgave her parents, she served them as their caretaker. My mother was the matriarch, the eldest girl of nine. She was amazing in so many ways -- generous to the bone. In 2003, my grandfather, the one who had abused her all those years before, called and asked her to quit her job, move across the country and take care of him and my grandma. She did, without hesitation. She endured his continually abusive words some 40 years later and served them for seven years. Honestly, I struggled watching her. But God sustained her and she held no grudge -- she had total forgiveness towards him. Recently, I was going through some of the last boxes of my mom's and I found a letter of forgiveness to her uncle for the sexual abuse that he had done to her as well.

I can testify that Mom's suffering has not been in vain. She dedicated her life to the Lord in her 50's and worked for Charisma Magazine and Joyce Meyers Ministries, touching many lives. Because of Jesus, just in my life alone, hundreds and hundreds of people have been touched, saved, healed and delivered. My daughter also belongs to Jesus and is finishing college now. My next book will be about the structure of abuse -- the demonic nature of abuse and how to break off the demonic structure that comes in with this exploitation. Who knows all that has yet to happen in God? The Lord showed me that we can never "outgive" God. Whatever we give Him, our sacrifices never ever go unnoticed. He will always bring blessings out of our sacrifices, even our sacrifices in tragedy! On April 9th of 2014, in my mother's last moments on the earth, I shared with her that I would never ever forget the sacrifices that she endured to enable my daughter, my brother, my niece and myself to exist. It was not in vain!

Again, when faced with pain and suffering, we often want to put God on trial and say, "Why God? Why did you allow this to happen?" However, I challenge us with this. Since God is the supreme Sovereign Being and Creator of all things, Ruler over all, having His creation put Him on trial as if He is answerable to us is probably not the best approach to take (and it doesn't work either!). God will never answer to us. It is only through humility that we can approach Him. James 4:6 states, *"...God opposes the proud but shows favor to the humble."*

However, as His creation, we are here to learn daily and grow more Christ-like in our walk. What if we ask, "Lord, what am I to learn from this situation? What about God and His nature can I only learn through this specific circumstance? What can I learn about myself that I wouldn't learn in any other situation?" There is a facet of who Christ is that He wants to reveal to you, here and now, in this situation; a facet of Himself that you can only get to know in this particular sequence of events. This is a divine opportunity! Take advantage of this time and begin to see from heaven's perspective! Begin to relish this time of growing.

This approach works because we are in proper alignment; a state of humility, a place of waiting and learning. God's heart hurts when we hurt. He feels our pain and sorrow. He desires to reveal Himself to us. He delights in bringing forth revelation and healing to His children. We have to put ourselves in a position of clean hands and pure hearts to hear and receive what the Lord wants to reveal. (Ps. 24:3-4, Prov. 4:23, Mat. 5:8)

Lastly, the hardest time I ever had in offering forgiveness to someone was to myself. When I was 18 I had an abortion. When I came to know the Lord and was in a trusting, loving relationship with Him, He brought me face-to-face with my abortion. He said to me, "You murdered your child." I cringed, cowering in my own shame, guilt and condemnation. The truth was out! It wasn't a blob of tissue like I had dictated to myself. The lie I had repeated over and over as my mantra was all shattered in a matter of seconds. When God speaks, you **know** that it is Him! His voice reverberates in your soul! The embarrassment, humiliation, and mortification I felt can't be expressed here. As I confessed, "Yes, I have sinned. I murdered my child.", the sobbing began. The level of stripping and the beginning of the depths of healing that ensued were miraculous. You see, the demons of murder, rage, and hate all entered my soul as I laid on that abortionist's table and they sucked the life of my child out of me. That's when I felt demons enter my soul. No longer were they hidden. God just laid them bare, exposed, as I repented for my sins. He said, "You have to forgive yourself". He had forgiven me, but I now must choose to forgive myself. I thank God that day for my small group that loved me through that moment in life. It was the hardest thing I'd ever had to forgive. BUT GOD! The Lord showed me a vision of my son. His name is Mark, and God has totally and completely healed me from that experience.*4

No matter how difficult the situation, our part is choosing to forgive. **The Cross, the Blood, and the Name of Jesus will take you through it, heal you in it, and reveal more of Him to you!** The Gospel is a <u>Gospel that transforms</u> when we repent and forgive. That is the essence of the Gospel; it is the POWER of the Gospel and it is the TRUTH of the Gospel. <u>The Good News is -- in Him we have</u>

forgiveness of sins.

We can literally pray right now. Receive these words into your heart. I recommend saying them out loud to yourself and receiving them so that healing will sink deep into your psyche and soul. The promise of forgiveness releases us from spiritual bondage and can heal our bodies from disease. It has also been scientifically proven that emotional issues of the heart have spiritual roots that can lead to sicknesses and diseases. As we read earlier in James 5:16, we confess so we may be healed.

*My PRAYER for you…*

*I pray your heart be tender towards the will of the Father and that you offer up forgiveness to those who often don't deserve it. Because Jesus first loved us, we can receive His grace to extend what we are not able to without His help. Lord, loose your gift of grace to my friends now to forgive all those who have sinned against them, in Jesus' name. Lord, I pray an extra measure of grace for my friends to forgive themselves of all the sins they have committed against others and themselves in Jesus' name. Amen!*


## Prayer Point - Forgiveness

*1 I will speak as a voice for whoever hurt you and cannot say it to you directly now. I stand in proxy for them, saying this to you. Speak this out loud to receive it for yourself, as I say it to you.

**I Son/Daughter, am sorry where I failed you, disappointed you, rejected you, abused you, hurt you, betrayed you, lied to you, and abandoned you. Wherever I wounded you, I am so sorry. I was selfish and sinned against you. I was wrong. Please forgive me. I break off all the negative words I have spoken into your ear-gates**

and into your heart, and any physical pain I have caused. I ask that the Blood of Jesus cleanse them from you and the harvest of their fruits to be rejected, renounced and healed in your soul."

**Repeat this out loud.**

Jesus, I ask for your grace to pray this. Jesus, I choose by an act of my will to forgive (names) _____. I can't carry this pain, hurt, heartache of unforgiveness anymore. I nail it to the Cross where You paid for it. Lord Jesus, forgive me for my sin responses of _____ in reaction to these sins against me. I forgive them and myself. I cleanse all sicknesses in my body that unforgiveness has held my body captive to. I declare I be released and healed in my mind, body, and soul now through the blood that was shed on my behalf in Jesus' Name.

**Prayer Point - Judgment**

\*2 **Definition of Judgment: the right of passing sentence.**

> *Hebrews 12:15* "*See to it that no one comes short of the grace of God; that no root of bitterness springing up causes trouble, and by it many be defiled.*"
>
> *Matthew 7:1-2* "*Do not judge least you be judged yourselves for in the way you judge, you will be judged; and buy your standard of measure, it shall be measured to you.*"
>
> *Galatians 6:7* "*Do not be deceived, God is not mocked; for whatever man sows, this he will also reap.*"

If I had to teach only one thing, it would be about judgments. Many people have been snared in the trap of judgments. Judgments are one of the primary sins in all relationships; that is why they ensnare so many of us in their traps. One thing that can serve us well in life is to understand the law of judgment. The law of judgment is a truth like gravity is a truth. No matter how you throw something in the air, the law of gravity will always bring it back down. Judgments are similar; they function like a boomerang, except upon return the force of impact is exponentially increased!

## Judging

When we decide that we know better than another, we place ourselves on the throne of life, thus judging a situation and deeming ourselves the authority over the matter. This throne is a place reserved only for Jesus; it often is associated with a place of pain, injustice, or ego. Often, our first judgments are made when we are very young, and are typically against our parents. (Deut. 5:16) Judgments always perform like a boomerang. They go out and always come back. However, they manifest in our life with amplified and exponential force! Think of it like throwing out a snowball, but when it returns you get hit with a 12 lb. bowling ball instead! Judgments meted out come back with interest due because it is a sin and a spiritual law. The longer a judgment remains, the more its harvest grows. It is attached to the spiritual law of sowing and reaping. There are always consequences for sin. Here are some examples. 1) You judged your teacher as harsh and you reap a leader or boss that says, "all your co-workers think you're harsh". 2) You've judged your mother that she is fat and lazy and you reap a wife who is struggling to lose weight. 3) You have judged an employer as mean and without understanding. You seem to have people at church speaking about you, how mean and difficult you are and how you lack understanding. 4) You judge your dad, when you are twelve, as no good, lazy, worthless, a man who is always broke. (In your eyes, He refuses to work, help with housework, there is never money to do anything and he is always hurting your mom). You are now 24 years old, in a serious relationship or married, and your partner has turned into that exact same kind of person you vowed (which also needs repented of as well) you would *never* be with. I minister to people every day with stories like these.

The best way to determine if you have any judgments against someone is to write a letter (you never intend to send) to that person. What are your feelings toward them? Don't hold anything back. Write it all down. Leave it for a while. Come back to it a week later and read it. See where in the letter you have called them names (this is a sign of a judgment), accused them of things without factual personal proof (another sign). Phrases like, "you are so stupid", "how could you", "you are a selfish grinch" or "the hospital killed my daughter". Judgment = judged them dumb, selfish and mean. Then you reap someone in your current life saying that about you. This can happen with families, work places, politically or even in church.

You are reaping a harvest of what you have sown in judgment, which goes forward into your future generations! But Jesus! When we **repent** for taking God's place in judgment, forgive the person we have judged, and **break** the harvest (interest) of that judgment off ourselves and future generations, it is broken off **by the Blood of the Lamb** and the authority of the believer! Amen! God always makes a way of escape for those who are obedient. The bible says my people perish for lack of knowledge. It is so true. We must learn the promises of the Kingdom provided by Him to us, for our protection and fulfillment.

### Prayer Point – Judgment (Matthew 7)

**Dear Lord Jesus, I repent for pride and for sitting in Your place on the throne of my heart. Show me any judgments that I have made.** *Wait on the Holy Spirit to reveal them to you.*

I repent for judging _____ (name) for my response of _____ (action).

I choose, by an act of my will, to forgive them for _____.

I renounce the judgment of_____. I surrender them to You for your vengeance, Lord. (Romans 12:19) _____.

I ask your forgiveness for my judgment and I take myself off the throne and surrender to Your judgment and headship.

Jesus, I ask You to take Your place in my heart.
I receive forgiveness and I loose this person to Your care. Your Word says, vengeance is the Lord's.
I break the judgments now, in Jesus' name.
I break the harvest of my judgments now, in Jesus' name, off of me and my children and grandchildren to the 3rd and 4th generations.

I receive God's commandment for me to love and I ask you, Lord to restore all relationships. I receive Your blood to cover my wrongful judgments. Help me to love more, love deeper, love greater. Help me to love, Lord, as You love. May the promises of Your Love, Joy and Grace replace my judgments! Amen.

> *Matthew 5:33-37. Again, you have heard that the ancients were told, "You shall not make false vows, but you shall fulfill your vows to the Lord." but I say to you, make no oath at all, either by heaven, for it is the throne of God, or by the earth, for it is the footstool of his feet, or by Jerusalem, for it is the city of the great King. Nor shall you make an oath by your head, for you cannot make one hair white or black. But let your statement be,*

*"Yes, yes, "or "No, no"; and anything beyond these is of evil.*

**Definition of Inner Vows - a determination set by the mind and heart into all the being, often in early life. It ties the person to the declaration spiritually and the biblical law produces its result. Inner vows are usually identifiable with the words, "I'll always" or "I'll never".** Scripturally we are told not to make vows we can't keep because a vow is an oath to God. Being created in God's image, when we make a vow our voice also has the power to create. Vows are legal and binding spiritual decrees that also work within the law of sowing and reaping. When we vow anything, we are declaring a spiritual oath that God did not sanction (exception - Holy Sacraments). Therefore, we are bound to that decree. We may not see the consequences for the vow until the set time it is activated, and it usually does not come forth right away. Think of it like this. We know that every person has a set time to die, but we don't know what the day or the hour of our death will be. Vows rest dormant until their stated time of activation, much like a coffee pot is programmed to turn on automatically at a set time. Our minds work much like electricity works. The power plant has lots of power, but the power can only run thru the lines provided to the house and has to follow the electric path, no matter where the owner wants the power to go. But there is no power in the house until someone turns on the switch to channel the power to the light bulb. When a vow is activated, it is like the power at the power station waiting for the timing of the power to be turned on at the switch. Then it has to follow the path that has been preset. As referenced earlier, there can be good and bad vows (any that aren't sanctioned by God are bad) that need release to bring freedom. Inner vows are stuck in the heart and aren't responsive to our wills. Only the spiritual authority of repentance through the Blood of the Lamb will free us from these.

Prayer Point – Inner Vows

**Dear Lord Jesus, I ask You to reveal any ungodly vows I have made in my childhood. Any place where I vowed not to be like my parents, or vows I made because of the situations I was placed in. I choose to forgive them. Where did I vow that I would never_____ or I'll always _____? I wait on you, Holy Spirit to reveal them to me now.** *(Many religions, college sororities, clubs, freemasons, etc. request you make vows. Some may seem good, for instance a vow to a church. That is not good and it needs to be repented.* **I repent for vowing that I _____. I ask forgiveness for making that vow against Your Word to not make vows. I renounce the vow that I _____. I break the vow with the Blood of the Lamb shed for my sins. I receive forgiveness. I forgive myself. I command my mind, will, emotions soul and body back to its original design and intent to produce life and to respond to the promises and benefits of the Word of God.**

*3 Statistics about sexual violence - National Sexual Violence Resource...
www.nsvrc.org/.../publications_nsvrc_factsheet_media-packet_statistics-abo...

One in 5 women and one in 16 men are **sexually assaulted** while in college (i). Rape is the most under-reported crime; 63% of **sexual assaults** are not reported to police (o). Only 12% of child **sexual abuse** is reported to the authorities (g). The prevalence of false reporting is between 2% and 10%.

*4 If you have suffered from an Abortion or are abortion-minded or know someone who is, you can find more resources on my website at: www.cherylweaver.org

or contact me at: Info@theresmoreministries.com.

www.RamahInternational.org Post- Abortion Recovery

## The Word Became Flesh II

A thought pondered creates an Idea
An Idea created reaps a revelation
A revelation conceived births a concept

A concept birthed without His Word reeks deception
Deception unchecked crafts lies as truth

Falsehood breeds a broad path of justification
Self-denial knows NO sin

Where there is sin – the flesh rules and the devil wins
Therein lies one word with a wide road of destruction
at its END

*Rev. Cheryl Weaver*
*September 2009*

## CHAPTER NINE
# THE PROMISE OF OVERCOMING

Overcoming temptations and generational bondages

Temptation is an evil that has to be overcome! As believers we are called "overcomers" because there are evil temptations to take the easier path. The path well-travelled verses the narrow road or the highway of holiness. Temptation comes to all believers; we WILL be tempted! When we are growing and deepening our walk to another level of self-sacrifice, we come into the wilderness of temptation. We need Jesus to reveal God's glorious grace to overcome three things: the wicked one, the flesh and our soulish nature. None of these entities like to be told "NO" -- not the devil, the flesh, nor the soul. However, as we choose to stand up against the bombardment of our soul from temptation, we grow stronger and the "overcomer" within us grows. We overcome by the Blood of the Lamb and the word of our testimony and not loving our lives unto death. That is obedience! "It's not by might, nor by power, but by My Spirit," says the Lord. When we are weak, He is strong in us!

What is the enemy's purpose of temptation? It is to undermine the will and plan of God in our lives (Gen. 3:4-5); to get us to lose our way and abandon our post (John 10:10). At its origin, it is to undermine God's authority, baiting us to declare our independence. However, the Word is alive and gives us declarations that have power in them to project the tempter of our soul out of our way!

In the wilderness, Jesus spoke to Satan. He stated, "Get behind me, Satan. It is written." Why didn't He say, "I said", or have God speak and say, "Leave Him alone."? Jesus, in this passage, was full of the Holy Spirit and the Spirit had led Him into the wilderness. Have you ever been led somewhere by God with one expectation only to find that His idea was quite different than your idea of what that time was going to be about? God has a purpose in allowing the enemy to tempt us. I believe it's because He wants us to understand that we have access to the same power as Jesus -- because Jesus is the Word in the Flesh! (John 1:14) So His (Jesus') flesh overcomes IN our flesh! Let me say it again -- His sinless flesh rose up and dismissed Satan's luring and His FLESH on the Cross now has given our redeemed flesh the grace to say "NO" when we face our wilderness experiences. A passage in Romans comes to mind:

> **Romans 5:17**
> *The sin of this one man, Adam, caused death to rule over us, but all who receive God's wonderful, gracious gift of righteousness will live in triumph over sin and death through this one man, Jesus Christ. Also He Suffered temptation and won, so He could help those tempted (Heb. 2:18).*

As I type this, I see a vision of Jesus standing up and His arms are open wide, inviting us into Him. He is welcoming us to come into deeper waters with Him, which enables us to hear Him more clearly and opens the door towards our overcoming. There are principles (promises) in the Word that give us strategies on how to activate and appropriate the Word into our daily lives; they give us the promise of liberty, freedom and peace through living the Word.

Temptation can steal our peace. Where is this reaction to temptation rooted in man? The scripture says that there is a threefold temptation that befalls mankind.

Threefold temptation of man (Gen. 3:6; 1 Jn. 2:15-17)

1. Lust of the flesh
2. Lust of the eyes
3. The pride of life

The goal of the enemy when tempting Christ was threefold:
1) He wanted to provoke Jesus to respond in the flesh for and from Himself, independent of His Father. (Lust of flesh)
2) Satan wanted Jesus to prove He was the Son of God. (Pride)
3) He offered up the rulership of this world, Satan's dominion (that Christ already had dominion over), in exchange for Christ's bowing His knee to worship him. (Lust of the eyes - John 18:36)

Here are some scriptures that help us understand how the structure of temptation furthers the enemy's goals, and how we can guard against it.

1. First, let us not harden our hearts. If our hearts are unclean and hardened to hearing God, we are more apt to fall into temptation.

    ***Psalm 95:8 (KJV)***
    *8 Harden not your heart, as in the provocation, and as in the day of temptation in the wilderness:*

    ***Hebrews 3:8 (KJV)***
    *8 Harden not your hearts, as in the provocation, in the day of temptation in the wilderness:*

2. Second, when we encounter adversity, we are more apt to be tempted. When we as believers are weakened in our resolve, down and in despair, the enemy targets us in those moments.

> *Matthew 6:13 (KJV)*
> *13 And lead us not into temptation (adversity), but deliver us from evil: For thine is the kingdom, and the power, and the glory, forever. Amen.*

3. It is easy for those of wealth and means to fall into the snare of temptation. Anyone who gives into foolishness and hurtful lusts of the flesh is susceptible to destruction as well.

   > *1 Timothy 6:9 (KJV)*
   > *9 But they that will be rich fall into temptation and a snare, and into many foolish (sensual) and hurtful (injurious) lusts, which drown men in destruction and perdition.*

4. The Word advises us multiple times to be diligent to watch and pray, be alert, stay awake, don't be dulled down, be ready to rise up and declare our petitions; being ever mindful and praying earnestly, worshipping the Lord Jesus. This will keep us from falling prey to temptation. If the Lord repeats Himself, it's IMPORTANT! **When maintaining our daily relationship, it's not as easy to fall prey to temptation.**

   > *Matthew 26:41 (KJV)*
   > *41 Watch and pray, (be alert, vigilant, worship and make petition) that ye enter not into temptation: the spirit indeed is willing, but the flesh is weak.*

   > *Mark 14:38 (KJV)*
   > *38 Watch ye and pray, lest ye enter into temptation. The spirit truly is ready, but the flesh is weak.*

   > *Luke 22:40 (KJV)*
   > *40 And when he was at the place, he said unto them, Pray (earnestly worship and petition) that ye enter*

*not into temptation.*

> **Luke 22:46 (KJV)**
> *46 And said unto them, why sleep ye? Rise and pray, lest ye enter into temptation.*

5. To keep ourselves from falling into temptation, we have to be rooted and grounded in the Word of God so that we will not fall away in unbelief during hard times. We are not to be like the good seed that falls on rocky ground and springs up quickly, yet has no root to survive difficulty.

> **Luke 8:13 (KJV)**
> *13 They on the rock are they, which, when they hear, receive the word with joy; and these have no root, which for a while believe, and in time of temptation fall away.*

6. Repentance and forgiveness is the Gospel of the Kingdom. We must be able to repent for our wrongs and confess our sins. In addition, we have to forgive those who wrong us. This is the key to keeping a clean heart and pure hands. As we do this, it helps prevent us from being led into temptation.

> **Luke 11:4 (KJV)**
> *4 And forgive us our sins; for we also forgive every one that is indebted to us. And lead us not into temptation; but deliver us from evil.*

7. God is a good God and He will not give us more than we can bear. Jesus came, as we stated earlier, **suffered temptation and WON! His grace is sufficient for us and helps make a way of escape!** When you find yourself in the midst of the battle: first, resubmit yourself to the Lord; second, worship and prayerfully surrender; third, ask for grace to resist declaring, "I

resist the enemy's temptation and take a stand!". Stand firm. When Satan knows that you know who you are in Jesus, He flees at that moment!
In James 1:14-15, the scripture tells us the story of how the process of temptation ensnares us.

> **James 1:12-16 (KJV)**
> 12 Blessed is the man that endureth temptation: for when he is tried, he shall receive the crown of life, which the Lord hath promised to them that love him. 13 Let no man say when he is tempted, I am tempted of God: for God cannot be tempted with evil, neither tempteth he any man: 14 But every man is tempted, when he is drawn away of his own lust, and enticed. 15 Then when lust hath conceived, it bringeth forth sin: and sin, when it is finished, bringeth forth death.

We are *tempted* with thoughts of evil.
Then we are *drawn* away with strong imagination.
*Lust* looms, and we delight in viewing it.
This gives way to *enticement,* weakening the will.
Lust then is *conceived*, and we yield to it.
Sinful action is taken resulting in submitting to *sin*.
The result of sin is *death*.

James 1:16 admonishes us, "Do not err, my beloved brethren." Meaning, do not be deceived. Evil consumes its prey. The path to destruction is wide, narrow is the gate that leads to life.

As we endure in patience, waiting for the deliverance of the Lord with our eyes fixed on Him, He will keep us through the hour of temptation that is coming upon the world in the last days. Do you know you have that kind of power in the Blood of Jesus? Because you do! When we experience this kind of temptation and we stand firm and hold steady, God's promise to us is to bless and reward the faithful with a crown of life! Many have seen in the Spirit the crowns that others have and are wearing in Heaven.

> ***1 Corinthians 10:13 (KJV)***
> *13 There hath no temptation taken you but such as is common to man: but God is faithful, who will not suffer you to be tempted above that ye are able; but will with the temptation also make a way to escape, that ye may be able to bear it.*
>
> ***James 4:7-8 (KJV)***
> *7 <u>Submit</u> yourselves therefore to God. Resist the devil, and he will flee from you.*
>
> ***Luke 4:13 (KJV)***
> *13 And when the devil had ended all the temptation, he departed from him for a season.*
>
> ***James 1:12 (KJV)***
> *12 Blessed is the man that endureth temptation: for when he is tried, he shall receive the crown of life, which the Lord hath promised to them that love him.*
>
> ***Revelation 3:10 (KJV)***
> *10 Because thou hast kept the word of my patience (hopeful endurance, patiently waiting), I also will keep thee from the hour of temptation, which shall come upon all the world, to try them that dwell upon the earth.*

I praise God that He is the Keeper of our souls and that He first loved us; He came and rescued us from utter destruction. If you haven't met the Lord who loves you in ways your earthly father never could, then I encourage you to ask Jesus to come into your heart. Ask Him to become your Father and Friend that will never leave you or forsake you, and find a divine peace, hope, and love you have never known. It is experiencing His true love for you that will keep you and guard you. Applying these lessons from the Word will enable you to continue to fight the good fight of faith and not fall prey to the lusts of the flesh that derail us from our true purpose and destiny!

Temptation rarely comes in a quick, easily identifiable package when things are going well and you are on the mountaintop. Make no mistake it can that way, but it rarely does. Satan is subtle and sneaky and worms his way into our lives little by little. By the time we notice him, we are usually in the danger zone. Satan asked God if he could sift Peter. He also asked God to take away Job's hedge of protection. These two examples in scripture show us that Satan is still subject to God and must ask permission of Him, then can only do what he is allowed. God uses the enemy for His ultimate plans toward bringing good.

Lessons in theory are great for learning, but I have found in life that practical application tends to be a better teacher and the Lord knows what we need and when we need it. So I would like to share a personal story of utter failure and God's faithful redemption regarding temptation. It is one of my absolutely, uttermost, moral failings with God, my husband and myself. You see, temptation is always birthed out of lust; lust for self, pride, lust for things and even a lust for self-preservation.

First, a bit of background. When I received Jesus, I was the first in four generations of my family bloodline to come into the fullness of all God had for us. My mom was one of nine children, born second eldest and the first girl. I had one aunt that had been saved when she was young, as the remnant or tithe of the family! I praise God for her and her prayers for our lineage. I am the first fruit from her prayers. God stopped the cycle of generational sins and demonic structures in my family lines with me. The Word states, "The sins of the father go to the fourth generation." Remember, my mom was five when she sat on Jesus' lap and discussed coming back to life to give birth to her children and grandchildren because they had an assignment. I didn't learn of that experience until years later. But I did learn about the generational curses the hard way as a young believer.

Now for the rest of the story! In 1990, Wayne and I were married, moved to a new city and received the Lord -- all in the same year. We were trying to grow as a couple, and as Christians, that first seven years. It was quite a challenge for us. There were many vows, judgments, generational curses, and our own fleshly sins that we were breaking through and getting free from on a weekly basis.

Jumping forward to year seven, Wayne and I had been living like roommates by that time and our marriage wasn't functioning. We were not engaging in the relationship and we both were operating in selfish ways. I was working as a Marketing Representative for a major mall and started noticing that others were attracted to me (I was tempted and drawn). Because I wasn't getting noticed at home, this opened a doorway (I was enticed) and that was the day that I began to be led down the pathway to death. As months progressed and I engaged this enticement (I yielded), I found myself slowly fascinated with the pleasure of my own desires growing stronger (sin acted out). I moved out and found an apartment and ended up having an affair. Wayne had seen in the Spirit the word "Adultery" written across my forehead. The Lord had revealed it to him in a vision. What would make me do such a thing? Yes, I was a Christian. I would cry out daily, "Lord don't take your Spirit away from me".

In my seven years of learning about Jesus, never once in any of the three churches I attended did anyone teach on "Character" and that being a Christian means you must have character and integrity. That is one of the reasons for writing this book, to help others see the importance of character before they fall prey to the wiles and schemes of the evil one and to share that God is faithful even when we are not.

I was tempted and I didn't say "NO". At the time, Wayne and I were under the influence of demonic powers pulling us towards evil. We didn't know that the evil had control over us. I had spent the first seven years of my marriage working day and night (repenting, breaking cycles, and learning about dysfunction) so I would not repeat my parent's marriage. (When I was very little, my father would pick me up and use me as a human shield to protect himself from my mom throwing knives or hammers at him. As I grew up with my parents, fighting was common. My brother and I encountered pickle jars and pots of beans being thrown between them over the dinner table, Pepsi being sprayed at each other – usually it would end with me cleaning up the mess.)

Here is a bit more background on Wayne and myself. My husband had grown up with a single mom and two younger brothers. His dad walked out when Wayne was eight years old. My husband took on the role of substitute mate (taking on responsibilities) as the oldest boy and without a father in the home. We both dealt with forms of parental inversion growing up. I had both parents, but one was emotionally checked out. (I had judged my dad as weak and my mother was very strong, but both my parents walked in parental inversion with me. I had been taking care of them since I was very young in various ways. Both parents being children of adult alcoholics and codependent, they raised us the same. It was the only way they knew how to function.) My mom's family suffered under a severe structure of sexual and alcohol abuse. This abuse structure carries with it rape, rage, molestation, adultery, lust, fornication, perversion, control, witchcraft, Jezebel and a whole lot more. That entire structure was still alive and lying in wait to snare me that day of my intrigue. I struggled my whole life with lust and when things at home were not working, Satan found his opportunity to loose the bait of temptation. I took it hook, line and sinker.

The generational sins in our families had never been released. I met with a family member of Wayne's and found out that the first seven years of our marriage was a repeat pattern of his parent's marriage, line-upon-line, precept-upon-precept. I had spent all that time breaking off the curses of my parent's marriage, but I never thought to break the curses off of my in-law's marriage. Because Wayne was in the role of substitute mate when he was younger, that curse (role) kicked back in subconsciously when we married. He kept seeing me as his mother, not his wife. Therefore, things drastically changed from our dating life to our marriage life. I was no longer a woman he desired to romantically cherish, I was a helper (mother figure) who gave instructions. He was no longer my lover, he was my roommate and I was being driven into needing more and more affection by the lust of my soul and my generational propensity toward evil. I was driven by the demons of lust, fornication, and adultery. I was fighting four generations of lust addictions. It was the perfect demonic storm -- BUT GOD! God knew before we were born and before we said, "I Do", the challenges we would face. Where we fail, HE IS FAITHFUL!

Three months after I left Wayne, the Lord spoke and said to me, "If you don't go home today, you won't have a home to go home to." I went home, became accountable to my small group, repented, and renounced and expelled (puked up) many demons over the next few months. The Lord allowed us to walk through this horrible situation to expose the demonic generational bondages and the structures we were under so we could tear down generations and generations of strongholds that were in both our families' lineages.

### *Exodus 20:5-6 (KJV)*
*[5] Thou shalt not bow down thyself to them, nor serve them: for I the LORD thy God am a jealous God, visiting the iniquity of the fathers upon the children unto the third and fourth generation of them that hate me; [6] And*

*shewing mercy unto thousands of them that love me, and keep my commandments.*

Satan wanted to tear us apart and prevent my mother's grandchild from coming into the earth, but God used it for His Glory. The Spirit of God's grace and healing was upon us both. Our small group gathered around us and prayed fervently for months until we were delivered of all the demons, lies, curses, vows, and judgments we had made. These bondages were keeping us from being able to be successful as husband and wife. Dying to self is the most important lesson we can learn in Christ, and also in marriage. The sooner we choose to die and prefer one another, the faster and deeper our relationship will grow with each other and in Christ. We will become healthy and bearing much fruit. Wayne did that for me, entering into the sufferings of Jesus, carrying my sin and pain against him to the Cross. I honor him for that. It took about two years for Wayne and I to be fully restored. Praise God, He is faithful! When we are weak, He is strong! God's Spirit will give you power to say "NO" when you resubmit yourself to Him as James 4:7 states.

**Philippians 3:10 (KJV)**
*10 That I may know him, and the power of his resurrection, and the fellowship of his sufferings, being made <u>conformable</u> unto his death;*

Our marriage today is better than ever and our hearts are one. We have grown so much over the years in God's wisdom and understanding. We have been set free of MUCH! The love we have for one another is unconditional and God has taught us how to communicate in each other's love language and to meet our needs. I have been faced with many additional temptations along these lines over the years and the Lord delivered me of the curses and the propensity to fall into evil. He has given me His grace to overcome the temptations as I have submitted to Him. He gave Wayne and I wisdom on how to set up boundaries to protect ourselves.

God created marriage between one man and one woman before the fall in the Garden of Eden. Therefore, it is my philosophy that we shouldn't settle for anything but the greatest relationship that He created, pressing through the obstacles for God's heavenly design to be fulfilled!

If you or a loved one has fallen into the sins of sexual perversion, adultery, fornication, pornography and the like, God can intervene. He desires to heal, deliver and set you free. The key is to have a humble and contrite heart to quickly acknowledge your sin and genuinely repent. This takes great courage. God's grace is sufficient for you. Everything has to be brought to the light for true fullness of life, restoration and peace to come! Your repentance may not be accepted by man, but God forgives you. We pray man forgives you as well and that God will soften the hearts of those affected by your sin.

*My PRAYER for you…*

I pray for your heart to be guided by the Holy Spirit and that you will forgive yourself as well. If you were betrayed by someone, I pray your heart will be softened and that His grace will fill you to forgive as Jesus has forgiven you. May the Lord of lovingkindness bring you times of refreshing so that you may be renewed in heart, mind, body, and soul.

**PRAYER POINT**

**Dear Lord Jesus, I ask You to be my Savior, a true Father to me and a Friend. I thank You that You will never leave me nor forsake me and I ask for Your divine**

love, peace and hope that I have never known. I ask that Your love will keep me and guard me. Help me to apply these truths and promises to my life. Help me to walk upright in character and integrity, to fight the good fight of faith and accomplish my purpose and come into my true identity and destiny. Amen.

*See Resource section for prayer of renouncement, breaking of generational curses and breaking soul-ties (sexual/spiritual ties to anyone you're not married to)

UNBROKEN PROMISES

## ***CALVARY***

Lord, I celebrate the love You gave to me

Love You bestowed on Calvary

Lord, I celebrate the blood You poured out on me

Blood You shed on Calvary

Lord, I celebrate the salvation You paid for me

Salvation bought on Calvary

Lord, I celebrate the peace You delivered to me

Peace You released on Calvary

Lord, I celebrate the freedom You gained for me

Freedom You won on Calvary

Chorus
Lord, I celebrate
Lord, I celebrate
Lord, I celebrate
This day You rose from Calvary

*Betty Clinton*
*April 2, 1999*

# UNBROKEN PROMISES

## CHAPTER TEN
# PAIN AND THE PROMISE OF HIS PRESENCE

What does His presence have to do with pain? Everything! Whether you are experiencing the pain of a mental disorder, a physical disease, or grief due to a relationship, whatever the cause of your pain there is a solution towards healing -- it is His presence. The Word says in John 16:33, *"In this life you will have troubles, but take heart; I have overcome the world."* If we receive and believe what Jesus did for us on the Cross, then His benefits still apply today. His healing presence is a supernatural gift that has no expiration date!!

> ***Genesis 28:15 (ESV)***
> *Behold, I am with you and will keep you wherever you go, and will bring you back to this land. For I will not leave you until I have done what I have promised you."*
>
> ***1 Peter 2:24 (ESV)***
> *He himself bore our sins in his body on the tree, that we might die to sin and live to righteousness. By his wounds you have been healed.*

As we learned in an earlier chapter, our first response is to accept Him and welcome Him into our hearts to live. How do we do that? We simply respond by repenting for our wrongdoing (sin) and surrender by faith what we can't bear. We surrender it to the Cross, allowing Him to carry it for us. He will take it, if you give it to Him. Once you have received this free gift and welcomed Jesus into your heart you can ask the Lord, "What am I to learn? What am I to pray?" These questions are powerful when we are experiencing pain, sorrow, grief, or suffering in this life. Then, listen for His response! As we are obedient to do what He has shared with us, we can surrender emotional and physical pain, giving it to Him to carry and bear. We then receive His healing presence in exchange. Whether we are a brand new receiver of Jesus into our hearts or a long time believer, we are all simply learning the process of surrender, hearing and obedience. This is an essential element in processing painful situations.

Pain hurts! Everyone wants to avoid it. Everyone wants to run from anything that presents itself as hurtful. We avoid communication with people if we think it will cause pain. We put off going to the doctor if we think pain is involved. We divorce because we feel we can't take any more pain. As children and some adults, if we receive pain, we learn to channel it. Our memories can use a self-protection mode to deflect it, fragment it, and section it away for a later time. Why? Because we don't know how to deal with pain. They don't teach us that in school. By definition -- pain is physical suffering associated with a bodily disorder (such as a disease or injury) and accompanied by mental or emotional distress. Pain, in its simplest form, is a warning mechanism that helps protect an organism by influencing it to withdraw from harmful stimuli.

**Pain is a warning mechanism that causes us to withdraw from harmful environments.** So, we come by it honestly; we feel the heat of a stove, and we withdraw our hand. We sense someone is going to hurt us, so we avoid them. We see a policeman as we are driving and we slow down, because of perceived future pain in our wallet. What is the truest essence of that pain's purpose to the receiver? And how did this warning system come to be? Why would our bodies warn us in this manner, and how do we choose to respond to such warnings?

As human beings, we are *driven* by many things, but I believe that those "many" things can be funneled down to only a few: the desires of our bodies, the pride of our life and the envy of our eyes. You can be driven by any of these in positive or negative ways. For example, a person can be driven by greed, by gambling, or by climbing the corporate ladder. One might look at the gambler and view his activity as negative to our society but then look at the corporate climber and see him as someone who is doing well. Both, however, are driven by the same lust for selfishness, to fulfill a need, a void in their soul; the pride of the climb, the reward of the company car, the partnership, or the country club membership. **All of these things are fueled by one of two factors: inspiration or pain.** Either we are called to action by inspiration to be something else or to acquire something we don't have; or we are fueled by pain -- one of the two. The gambler goes to the tables to relieve his addiction or to receive a high to relieve the pain he has buried deep inside; it's the same for the drug addict, shopaholic, narcissist, etc., a temporary fix for the pain that is deep within. We use many things to make ourselves feel good, everything from overworking, to sex, to eating, to putting others down. Some try to fix people (a form of co-dependency) as their way of avoiding their own pain. The list goes on and on; there are many forms we use to relieve the pain and fill the void in our souls.

> **Mark 4:17 (BBE)**
> [17] *And they have no root in themselves, but go on for a time; then, when trouble comes or pain, because of the word, they quickly become full of doubts.*

So, the real issue here is that we need greater enlightenment and greater understanding of who God is! We need understanding of who God is in the midst of the pain, grief, or sorrow and what the "source" is that causes us this distress. The awesome thing about the God of the Universe is that He is a loving God that feels our pain with us. We are never alone. He is always with us.

> **Exodus 33:14 (ESV)**
> And he said, "My presence will go with you, and I will give you rest."
>
> **Jeremiah 29:13 (ESV)** You will seek me and find me, when you seek me with all your heart.
>
> **Psalm 139:7 (ESV)**
> Where shall I go from your Spirit? Or where shall I flee from your presence?
>
> **1 Corinthians 3:16 (ESV)**
> Do you not know that you are God's temple and that God's Spirit dwells in you?

When we approach him in humility and ask questions we can learn from, HE LOVES to respond to us. He loves to teach us more about who He is and who we are in Him. So again, it bears repeating, let us recognize the right questions to ask: "What can I learn from this pain and painful situation? What should my response be?"

Remember the definition of pain -- a warning mechanism to protect us. Why do we place babies in pack-n-plays? Because babies wander off and play with things that are dangerous and harmful; for example, an electrical socket is at a baby's height and could kill an infant. The Bible is God's Inspired Word providing us a protective manual, a set of "how to" instructions that allow us to live a happy and joyful life. This manual, written under the inspiration of the Holy Spirit of God and given to His creation, shows us the promises of His presence and the consequences if we go outside of those protective boundaries. Life outside these boundaries will cause us harm; God wants to provide us with the wisdom to live abundant, fruitful, healthy lives.

What is the Creator, in all His wisdom, doing for us? He has put in each of us a warning mechanism that tells us something is wrong physically, mentally, or spiritually! Pain is often due to something being off in our relationship with our Creator. One of my favorite scriptures is, *"Guard your heart for it is the wellspring of life." Prov. 4:23*

That pain was created as a warning mechanism to say "repent" for your wrongdoing (sin) and receive the free gift I have given you in my Son taking your pain (sin) on the Cross. We get a warning light, like when our car dash light blinks telling us we have a problem with the car. It is saying, "system engine check." God is saying to us, "system heart check"! What area of your life is not lining up with the truth that I say about you? The love I have for you? The blood My Son shed for you on the Cross to take your place of punishment? Someone has to pay the penalty for sin, the pain caused against us and the pain we cause - our wrongdoing (sin). Jesus did so to restore our relationship with the Father. God wants his entire family to be with Him and receive his blessings of healing presence -- love, joy, peace, and hope – and to enable us to walk in them continually.

> ***James 5:14-15 (ESV)***
> *Is anyone among you sick? Let him call for the elders of the church, and let them pray over him, anointing him with oil in the name of the Lord. And the prayer of faith will save the one who is sick, and the Lord will raise him up. And if he has committed sins, he will be forgiven.*
>
> ***Psalm 16:11 (ESV)***
> *You make known to me the path of life; in your presence there is fullness of joy; at your right hand are pleasures forevermore.*

The Father loves us and provided a way for us not to suffer under our own penalty of judgment for our wrongdoing. He does not want us to carry the burden of that pain, sorrow and suffering. He sent someone to take our place. His Son named Jesus! Jesus, who did nothing wrong in His 33 years of existence, God's holy Son, willingly got up on the Cross and took our punishment, our sickness, our pain and paid our penalty. We deserved the punishment for all we have done wrong in the past, present and future; yet, He took the beatings, ridicule, shame, guilt, pain, accusations, and sickness -- ALL PUNISHMENT. He took those who sinned against you and I, and He took our sin. He bore it in our place so we can now walk in peace, love, and hope; so we may forever be a part of God's family and possess eternal life.

> ***James 5:16 (ESV)***
> *Therefore, confess your sins to one another and pray for one another, that you may be healed. The prayer of a righteous person has great power as it is working.*
>
> ***Psalm 140:13 (ESV)***
> *Surely the righteous shall give thanks to your name; the upright shall dwell in your presence.*

Many believe that when we are in pain, God is not there; thus, they have surrender their faith to experience. Pain and experience NEVER negate the Word of Truth. However, we can elevate our experiences and pain above the Word. We, or our predecessors, through strongholds in the mind, judgments, curses, or vows can cause this. The Truth and the Word of God have to override our experience, which is our responsibility in the healing process.

Pain does not remove God's safety, intimacy, or relationship. Just because we have pain in our life does not mean that we don't have safety or that God has abandoned us -- quite the contrary. We have the Lord's attention. He is giving us a system alert. He promises in His word to comfort us and stick closer to us than a brother and bring healing to us. The God of the Universe, who created oceans, animals, and mountains, cares enough about each of us to know the number of hairs on our head and collect every tear we cry in a bottle! **Pain often lies to us,** and much of the time it is hard for us to receive while in a state of pain. Pain often conjures up a state of self-pity and no one can see or hear God when they are in a "state-of-self". We are always called to look up, beyond ourselves, and lean by faith on the One who created us. We are all designed to heal!

*3 John 1:2 (ESV)*
*Beloved, I pray that all may go well with you and that you may be in good health, as it goes well with your soul.*

*Matthew 11:28 (ESV)*
*Come to me, all who labor and are heavy laden, and I will give you rest.*

*Matthew 10:1 (ESV)*
*And he called to him his twelve disciples and gave them authority over unclean spirits, to cast them out, and to heal every disease and every affliction.*

*Jeremiah 33:6 (ESV)*
*Behold, I will bring to it health and healing, and I will heal them and reveal to them abundance of prosperity and security.*

*Isaiah 53:5 (ESV)*
*But he was wounded for our transgressions; he was crushed for our iniquities; upon him was the chastisement that brought us peace, and with his stripes we are healed.*

***Proverbs 4:20-22 (ESV)***
*My son, be attentive to my words; incline your ear to my sayings. Let them not escape from your sight; keep them within your heart. For they are life to those who find them, and healing to all their flesh.*

***Psalm 147:3 (ESV)***
*He heals the brokenhearted and binds up their wounds.*

***Psalm 30:2 (ESV)***
*O **Lord** my God, I cried to you for help, and you have healed me.*

We understandably get so focused on the pain and the delusion of it that, if we are not careful, we can begin to believe the lies of the enemy.

The three lies the enemy tells us:

1) God is not with us;
2) We are too weak to keep on fighting;
3) We are not making any (or enough) progress (not ready, not praying enough, not performing enough).

We forget we were created to heal and receive healing in Christ Jesus. It is God's design for us! In every physical situation our body was created to heal itself. A scab is the process of healing. Our red and white blood cells go into action to relieve our bodies of foreign objects, recognizing what doesn't belong in our bodies. As we emotionally heal from problems, we go through all six stages of human processing:

1) Denial
   Peter – Luke 22:61, Eve – Gen. 3:6,
   New Heart – Eze. 36:26

2) Anger
   Bitterroot- Heb. 12:15, Eph. 4:26,
   Response- Rom. 12:20-12, Eph. 4:32
3) Forgiveness
   Mat. 18:34-35, Col 3:13-14, Mk 11:25-26, Jam. 2:13, Acts 3:19-20
4) Depression
   (Guilt, Shame, Anxiety, Anguish, Bondage) David was Ps. 38, Relief Ps 32:57
5) Letting Go
   John 8:36
6) Acceptance
   Is. 25:8, 43:18-19, Rom. 8:28, 2 Cor. 1:3-4

If we don't go through all the stages, we get stuck and often physically ill. Kathie Walters (Minister of the Supernatural) and Bob Jones (Considered one of the fathers of the prophetic movement in this century) produced a book called, "Health Related Mindsets". Our ministry uses it faithfully when praying for the sick. It shares how physical sicknesses are most often rooted in spiritual conditions of the heart and soul.

When it comes to the soul, many don't understand that even death is the ultimate healing for a soul that has received Jesus as Savior. Heaven is a place where eternity is spent in bliss, love and joy with our Father who loves us. Death has no sting for a believer. It causes grief for loved ones, but to the individual, they are dancing on streets of gold and walking in the fullness of joy! However, for those who do not accept the free gift of Jesus' love and sacrifice on the Cross and have not received healing in their soul, they will not receive eternal life and will spend eternity in hell. They will live out eternity in a state of utter torment, because anyone who doesn't receive Jesus is automatically serving the god of this world, Satan, whether they worship him consciously or not.

> *2 Cor. 4:4 (NLT)*
> *Satan, who is the god of this world, has blinded the minds of those who don't believe. They are unable to see the glorious light of the Good News. They don't understand this message about the glory of Christ, who is the exact likeness of God.*

Much too often we have stopped leaning on God's design to heal us. We lean on our own understanding (Prov. 3:5). We are encouraged by Scripture to turn to Him first -- the Designer and Creator of our human form. Jesus is in heaven making intercessions on our behalf, the Word says. He hears the cries of His children. He is the lifter of our heads and His banner over us is love.

He is with us and He never leaves us nor forsakes us, like people often do. God is everything we wished our earthly fathers to be, but could not be. Remember, pain is a warning mechanism. It is not meant to be there forever. It alerts you that something is not working correctly, something is spiritually off in your heart and soul.

God will reveal where we need to insert His medicine of REPENTANCE and FORGIVENESS to remove the symptoms of pain and reap the benefits of TRUTH and HEALING into our situations. Then we can be recalibrated back into a pain-free, peaceful, and joyous state of being. As we seek Him and continue to apply His medicine of REPENTANCE and FORGIVENESS to every heartache, disappointment, betrayal, trauma, and loss that He reveals, then our pain can decrease. Sometimes this is a process. Sometimes this can be an overnight event. Once we are obedient to repent for our wrongdoings (sin) and response patterns, and forgive others and ourselves of wrongdoings (sins), the TRUTH will flood in and remove the lie. Then we can surrender the pain to the Cross and carry it no longer!

I would be remiss not to address that every sickness is not a consequence of our behavior or that of generations before us. However, I have over my many years of ministering healing to individuals, found a large number of correlations between heart attitude and healing issues. Nevertheless, one of the very essences of suffering is that it makes us more like Christ. Jesus never sinned and yet Christ suffered. Look at Job or Paul's lives. There is a place where we each have to pick up our cross and deny ourselves for the sake of the Kingdom and others.

> *1 Peter 4:12-19 (NIV)*
> *Dear friends, do not be surprised at the fiery ordeal that has come on you to test you, as though something strange were happening to you. 13But rejoice inasmuch as you participate in the sufferings of Christ, so that you may be overjoyed when his glory is revealed. 14If you are insulted because of the name of Christ, you are blessed, for the Spirit of glory and of God rests on you. 15If you suffer, it should not be as a murderer or thief or any other kind of criminal, or even as a meddler. 16However, if you suffer as a Christian, do not be ashamed, but praise God that you bear that name. 17For it is time for judgment to begin with God's household; and if it begins with us, what will the outcome be for those who do not obey the gospel of God? 18And, "If it is hard for the righteous to be saved, what will become of the ungodly and the sinner?" 19 So then, those who suffer according to God's will should commit themselves to their faithful Creator and continue to do good.*

"Learning to Suffer Well" is a book I read by Pastor Peter Fitch.* The essence of his message shares that we are molded into Christlikeness by our suffering; that in our patient endurance we learn about a facet of Christ that we could not learn elsewhere, trusting God in our pain. We all understand that we live in a fallen world, and that it is one source of suffering. A fallen world produces evil intent and selfishness, which creates harm. However, there is a kind of suffering that God induces ("...it is my good will to crush you." Is. 53:10) where our heavenly Father provides opportunities for wayward sons and daughters to come home to Him when they are faced with suffering and times of trial. Christ paid for Adam's mistakes. He is the second Adam to redeem us, bridging heaven to earth. We are praying for the life of heaven to be fulfilled here and now on earth, overcoming sickness, poverty and oppression. This is the promise we must activate by our agreement and wait in obedient faith to receive.

There are many ways God's healing presence comes through: by Jesus' virtue, the laying on of hands, anointing with oil, breaking off curses, deliverance, fasting, prayer cloths, prayer, and the Word! The Word is alive and it will not return empty but will accomplish the purpose for which it was sent.

God always makes a way of escape. I have found over the years that it can be a mystery that, at times, we have to pursue. However, anything worth having is worth the pursuit. It's often times in the journey that we find the answers and where we grow the most. If we were to have no valleys, we would not know the exhilaration of the mountaintops. This journey with God is always eventful and never boring. He loves you. He honors you and promises to bless you as you seek Him with all your heart, your entire mind and soul. I did, and it's been the most amazing ride of my life!

**PRAYER POINT**

**Dear Lord Jesus,**

**I dedicate myself to You and renounce any involvement with the occult, false religions and/or trauma that would**

blind my eyes from seeing You, and clog my ears from hearing You. I renounce all covenants made with them resulting in pain and suffering. I renounce any deaf and dumb spirits that are keeping me from receiving from the Lord. I repent for all previous generations of my bloodlines and their involvement, participations and covenants made. I ask forgiveness for myself and the sins of my bloodlines. I forgive them and I forgive myself. I renounce the spirit of trauma and pain, suffering, torment and false grief, off my body now in Jesus' name. I forgive the perpetrators of the trauma: _____ (list by name, even if it's yourself). I repent of my sin responses of: _____ (ill deeds, curses, judgments, vows etc.). I forgive myself. I come before You asking You to show me any other source or origin of my pain.

(Wait and listen for anything else.) Forgive, repent and release it to the Cross. I break all false covenants, judgments, vows, curses, hexes, vexes, jinx's, voodoo, witchcraft, now in Jesus' name. I break the harvest of those things off my life and my children and my children's children to 1,000 generations. I break any and all previous alliances or benefits of pain, suffering, trauma, false grief, and torment off myself and my bloodlines. I receive my bloodline blessings of fullness of life, healing, hope and peace of mind, body, soul and spirit for me and my children and my children's children to 1,000 generations. Amen.

\* If you have been suffering and have already walked out the processes we have discussed in this book, I highly recommend reading Peter Finch's book for deeper revelations on walking in the sufferings of Christ. *Learning to Suffer Well*, Peter Fitch ISBN 0-620-26375-X

## "This is My Lord"

### Song from the Book of Exodus

I will sing to my Lord
The Lord is my strength and my song
You are my salvation, oh Lord
Causing me to walk upon dry land
While in the midst of the sea

This is my Lord and I will praise Him
Who is like You, oh Lord?
Who is like You in holiness?
I will sing to my Lord
For He is highly exalted

The Lord is my Warrior
Jehovah is His name
Thy right hand is majestic, oh Lord
Awesome in it's power
Turning bitter water to sweet

This my Lord and I will praise Him
Who is like You, oh Lord?
Who is like You in holiness?
I will sing to my Lord
For He is highly exalted

I will sing to my Lord
As I entered the promised land
This place You made for me, oh Lord
With Your holy hands
Lord may You reign forever and ever

This is my Lord and I will praise Him

## CHERYL CLINTON WEAVER

Who is like You, oh Lord?
Who is like You in holiness?
I will sing to my Lord for He is highly exalted

*Betty Clinton*
*September 26, 1998*

## CHAPTER ELEVEN
# THE PROMISE OF LIFE

Holy Spirit verses Religion

The Holy Spirit lives in us, the same power that raised Jesus from the dead! (Rom 8:11) THINK ABOUT THAT! Do you understand that GOD HIMSELF LIVES IN YOU? (Rom 8:9, 11) Not a junior token gift, but the GOD of the Universe Who created the HEAVENS and THE EARTH with His WORD -- He gave YOU and ME the same Spirit to SPEAK LIFE into existence, taking dominion here on earth as His Voice, His Hands and His Feet! (Gen 1:26-28)

**We ARE because He IS!** I think we, the Church, downplay the Holy Spirit's role in the Trinity. Yes, He is the Comforter! He is the Helper! He is the Spirit that dwells within! Jesus was able to endure all He did because He was a MAN with that same SPIRIT within Him! The same Spirit that resisted the enemy in the wilderness. The same Spirit that led Jesus to the garden of Gethsemane, overcoming His own human flesh, to choose the will of the Father. Why? Because the SPIRIT of GOD living within Him enabled Him to walk out the will of the Father on the earth. This is the same SPIRIT that lives in you and me to accomplish ALL that He requests, and even greater, as we align our belief with His! (John 14:12)

Living, moving, and having our being in Him is the breath of ministry. Ministry, as I have shared with my team, is something that happens between you and the Lord. We were created to minister to our Lord and Savior first and foremost -- worshiping and being in relationship with Him is our first calling to ministry and truly, our only calling (Deut. 6:5). **It is**

**out of that place of ministry to the Lord through worship, adoration, and love between the Father and the son or daughter, that God releases a wake of gifts, anointing and fruit that will simply follow you everywhere you go.** As we adore the Father, He adores us and we can't ever outgive the Lord as we spend time with Him. He spends that time multiplying it back to us in love and changing us into His image. Thus, wherever we go and wherever we walk, (like Peter & Paul) our shadow has anointing to bring about changes in the atmosphere for Jesus, by Jesus and in Jesus! (Acts 5:15-16)

Ministry is the incredible revelation of this mystery of the Gospel on a daily basis. We worship and adore this all-powerful being who loves us so much that He placed Himself, the precious Holy Spirit, in these limited bodies to prove HIS limitless existence!!! YOU ARE HIS VISUAL AID ON THE EARTH. (Eph. 6:19-20)

*Ministry, in itself, is lifeless and limited when referred to by the title of a program.* I think we are sometimes confused on the concept of the subject matter of this broad and vast topic. Think about it. All our Christian life we hear about "ministry", "being in ministry", "doing the ministry". When it is relegated to anything outside of our personal relationship with our Love, King Jesus, *it is simply religion*! Let us not create a form or a structure and call that ministry! Ministry is not something we do, but it is a <u>by-product</u> of the NATURE of Christ being formed within our soul; the process of His limitless love being squeezed into our limited beings, consequently releasing abilities way beyond our fleshly carnal nature. The Spirit enables us to be here on the earth as "Christ's Ambassadors", loving beyond our ability, which then sets others free -- not by "doing", but by Him "BEING" in us! (Gal 4:19)

God is *L O V E*. Love covers and it knows no wrong. God is in you. We are one with Him. (1 John 4:8b) There is a circle of life that is released as we walk in the depth, breadth, width and height of that love. (Rom 8:39) In the process of the Spirit's overwhelming love, you can't help but love others. He changes your nature minute-by-minute as you embrace Him. His Love in you is a catalyst that is synergistically transforming all living things everywhere around you. This transformation is the process and nature of LIFE, complete from beginning to end. This happens by the Lord's pursuing love and nature being formed within the very soul of man. <u>The Gospel is a daily, transforming "truth". If you aren't being transformed, you don't have the true Gospel.</u>

**We (you and I) are the richest example of ministry as LIFE all around us is being transformed by the SPIRIT of love and selflessness in us.** His nature in us is being radically loosed on the people around us by the Spirit. This is Life! Life is who He is in us and who we are in Him -- it is organic. It's living fully in the Spirit applying the life Christ paid for. Life, and our ministry unto Him, is a verb, not a noun. It is a journey, not a destination. It is not a location in a building or an act that we perform for GOD. It's a dance of love weaving back and forth with the Father, understanding His heart in ours and our heart in His. This dance of releasing His nature on the earth radically reflects Him, and causes the world and all in it to enter into a dance themselves. That response becomes an organic movement, LIFE in the Spirit. Then the Father engages His other children because of the love you are loosing back towards the Father and then it's released over those in your path. He is a magnificent, limitless, powerful GOD, living in the very finiteness of our human condition and bringing Glory to Himself. MIRACULOUS!

Ministry isn't something we move towards, ministry isn't something we plan for, and ministry is not something we try to do, become, or fix. Ministry isn't a program or a strategy, it is a BY-PRODUCT of an everlasting, deep love affair with a

Savior who paid for everything you have ever done, everything you'll ever need and all that is in your future. Ministry isn't something that can be defined. How can you define GOD? Attempting to create something and call it a ministry is, in its very nature, already contrary to the very nature of Jesus and what He came to reveal on the earth.

Ministry in the day and time of Jesus was modeled in the Pharisees creating rules, regulations and stipulations "FOR GOD". This is much the same example or format of ministry we still see today in many places. We can have the best intentions. Take Saul, for example. His passion for God was unequalled, and yet he was blinded with self-righteousness. "Doing something for God" perverted the very nature and essence of Who God is -- **LOVE**. Jesus came to seek and save the lost, teaching us to love one another. We, like Saul, can be blinded by our desire to "DO" for God out of our lack of being "IN" God. The natural progression of "doing" for God is acts of performance. This gratifies our own desires and is completely devoid of the character of God himself, which is rooted in selflessness. Thus, we move into *"having a form of godliness but denying its power,"* walking in our own self-power to satiate the lust of the flesh. (2 Tim 3:5)

Yet our words and actions seem all so good on the outside and we are often blinded to the true motive of self-fulfillment. God is selfless. This is the hardest thing on earth to grasp. The nature of God in us is to be completely selfless and full of love. It is the purpose of our heavenly Father to create us as vessels that are utterly helpless in completing such a task without total and utter dependence on HIM, moment-by-moment and day by day. He longs for our relationship! Jesus was one with the Father, provoked by love, doing what HE heard the Father saying and obediently serving His will. We are also created to have the same response. (**Immediate, Radical, Costly, Obedient!**)

How much richer and fuller could our lives be if we were

moving and living and having our being in Jesus, motivated with the same heart intent that Jesus moved in towards the Father? (Acts 17:28) Life and life more abundantly! My exhortation to us today is that we are not called to FIX anything. **God is the Author and Finisher of our faith and He will complete what He has begun in us.** (Heb. 12:2, 1 Thess. 5:24) In Church ministry, when there is a problem, we create a program to fix it. Jesus went from village to village creating relationships, connecting people by His sacrificial obedience to the Father's love. (Matt 9:9, John 4)

Sacrificial giving and radical obedience is what we have to give our Father. It's a divine exchange we surrender to and He fills us with the greatest power on earth, the power of Life in the Spirit! There is nothing we can't accomplish while we are abiding in Him and Him in us. Life and fullness are in the abiding.

> ***Psalm 16:11 (NIV)*** *You make known to me the path of life; in your presence there is fullness of joy; at your right hand are pleasures forevermore.*
>
> ***John 1:16 (NIV)***
> *For of His fullness we have all received, and grace upon grace.*
>
> ***Romans 15:13 (NIV)***
> *Now may the God of hope fill you with all joy and peace in believing, so that you will abound in hope by the power of the Holy Spirit.*

We simply give back to him our life, worship and adoration. **When we share the testimony of all He is in us, it breeds change in others -- it is contagious, intentional love!** So let us be authentically recused from our human condition of carnality and become laid down lovers of Jesus, transforming a culture out of pure obedience to following after our Savior wherever He leads. I did and it's truly INTOXICATING!

My PRAYER for you...

*May the Lover of your soul and the Healer of your heart captivate you so radically that you totally abandon yourself to Him, fully and completely, being released into the greatest adventure you could ever have on Earth!*

**Prayer Point**

**Pray "Dear Lord Jesus, fill me with the Baptism of Your Spirit, full of Your love, abiding in the fullness of abundant life. Fill me with great grace to empower me to walk in radical, immediate, costly, obedience and receive the fullness of Your promises. Help me to see myself as You see me and to believe and receive the download of my full identity of heaven's persona of who I am in Jesus' name. I believe and I receive it. Amen.**

## ONE VOICE

One Voice gathered from many
One Body joined in harmony
To praise You, our Lord and King
Jesus, Jesus, Jesus
To worship You in unity

One Voice, one Body
We come together in Your Name
Streams of living waters
Jesus, Jesus, Jesus
We will never be the same

One Voice, one nation
Born again, transformed anew
To seek out all others
Jesus, Jesus, Jesus
To be a witness of You

One Voice lifted up in praise
To honor Your glorious Name
One Body, one nation
Jesus, Jesus, Jesus
We will never be the same

One Voice, one nation
We depend upon Your grace
Oh Lord, our God
Jesus, Jesus, Jesus
We seek Your radiant face

*Betty Clinton*
*February 25, 1999*

## UNBROKEN PROMISES

## CHAPTER TWELVE
# PERSEVERANCE TO THE PROMISE

I have a friend who is a personal trainer and he says, "You can have all the potential in the world, but unless you put that potential into action, it's still unfulfilled." Father Abraham persevered. The Apostle Paul was a man of perseverance. Christ Jesus, the Anointed One, persevered for all humanity. Dedication can be given verbally, but often is spoken just as a platitude offering. Commitment is a deeper level of understanding where you've agreed to be responsible for something and honor your word. However, perseverance is the deepest level of dedicated commitment promised through all difficulties and tribulations. Just as the saints of old, let us persevere in righteousness to the promises of God.

There are two kinds of perseverance -- one in self-effort and one within the Spirit of grace. Back in 2009, I was in a really hard place where everything went wrong, all in one week. The spiral began with my husband traveling out of the country. Then I lost my job. It was a great job. I was a Chaplain in a marketplace ministry witnessing to secular people and got paid for it. That week, my daughter Cassia, had just started back to school in the 6$^{th}$ grade. Then it happened! I opened the front door to step outside and our six year old registered, purebred Westie ran out the door, as he had many times before! Except this time, he didn't have his collar on. I ran and ran, chasing after him. He crossed our street and ran out onto the busy main thoroughfare. I was about 50 feet behind him. All of a sudden, a car on the main street slowed down, opened their car door while moving, and scooped up my daughter's puppy dog! "Robbie", her best friend (she is an only child), was stolen right from before my very eyes! We were in shock. I called the police but that was of no help. I paid for a service that called 250 of my neighbors, but no luck. My daughter and I made huge posters with Robbie's giant face on them. We went to the busiest intersection in town and held them up for all to see. Coincidently, there were other groups of people at the same intersection. They were soliciting money, but the police only addressed us and said, "You have to leave." We were the only ones that were not allowed to be there. We created "missing pet" flyers and stopped by dozens of veterinarians in town to post them. We put up flyers on every stop sign we could find. However, by the time we returned home, the flyers were mysteriously all laying in a pile at my doorstep, with a request we not put them up in the city!

I heard the Lord speak to me and say, "Stop looking for your dog". I said, "I can't. I feel like I lost my kid. I am hurting!" He said, "Stop looking for your dog." I continued the same steps again the next day and the day after. We had driven every day around the neighborhoods, fields, parks, and vet offices. Wayne was still overseas. I was angry that he didn't choose to come home to help us through this crisis. I was exhausted, angry, hurt, confused, and just about at my breaking point. The next day Cassia and I again placed flyers all over all the poles in the neighborhoods. Then the proverbial "straw that broke the camel's back" happened. Cassia and I were standing at a stop sign and the stapler stopped working and I lost it! I threw the stapler down, "yelling and cursing" God.

WHOA! Only milliseconds passed as I was profusely shocked at myself and repeatedly repented, "Oh my God, I am so sorry. Lord please forgive me, God I didn't mean it, I am so sorry." I got in the car and Cassia was sitting next to me and I kept repeating, "God I am so sorry, please forgive me." I went on and on like this for the next 15 minutes and finally my 12 year old said, "Mom, I think God heard you." I had been in ministry for years serving the Lord, but I was devastated! The Lord spoke to me in that moment, *"Cheryl, it is my good pleasure to crush you". (I found out later it was in the Word. Isaiah 53:10).* You may say, "Oh my, how awful!" And if you would have asked me that week, I would have agreed with you!

Nevertheless, God knows exactly what we need and when we need it. He knew that if He pushed all those different buttons (or circumstances) at the same time, that it would reveal what was in my soul. Something that I didn't know was still there -- rebellion! There was still a part of my soul that was hiding rebellion -- all my fleshly efforts of perseverance to create the circumstances that I wanted. In my blessed daily state of being, it was undetectable, but rebellion was hiding deep in my soul. The Lord exposed it for my good and His glory. The Bible states that rebellion is as witchcraft. It is evil and sin. God loves us and goes before us! He knew that even a little bit of rebellion in my soul would cause problems in my future and cause harm to others. Sin needs to be brought to the Light. My repentance and deliverance was required for the sake of my soul and for the witness of His personhood in me. Remember, in an earlier chapter I said, "hurt people always hurt people." Papa God didn't want me to carry that any longer and He didn't want it to show up later on in ministry, diverting destiny and causing damage to His people!

God's crushing is like that of crushing grapes; it is the process to get to the fine wine that you were originally intended to become. The righteous perseverance of grace that inspires me towards God was the root system that was already established to enable me to trust God when He spoke to me of His crushing. Trust me when I say you have to have His grace, a deep commitment of love and intimacy in relationship to hear Papa say what He said to Jesus, "It is my good will to crush you!". However, that is where trusting and knowing that Father God only has His very best in mind towards you and He never will let you go. Settling in your heart that Papa's intentions towards you are always, always, always to love, adore and bless you forward no matter what your circumstances look like -- that is the true test of righteous perseverance.

There is a place in each one of us that we will reach as we surrender to the Lord -- the breaking point of perseverance between human ability and God's grace-given ability. **One has to die so that the other can live.** We can't manage God. He is the One who is in charge. As long as we are pressing in our own directions and directives, we will never be able to walk in the fullness and limitless promise of the depths of our purpose. Praise God! He always gives us opportunities to learn and grow.

Years ago, I learned in small group training that there are four stages a group goes through when starting up: 1) Forming; 2) Storming; 3) Norming; 4) Performing. This is like our Christian journey with the Lord. He ministers to us in cycles, much like seasons. We have cycles and seasons that we walk in. When we are starting a new season, we are **forming** and finding our way in the season, learning to hear God in a new way and exploring our surroundings of the new season. Then He begins to show us all the areas of our life where we could use improvement -- a **storming** time exposing the ugliness of our hearts so that we will come to Him and be cleansed from our hindrances towards our next season. Then we fall down deeper into the cycle. We begin to start climbing the mountain of **norming**. We have identified how we are communing with the Lord, we have been cleansed and now we are moving forward in what we've learned. We are gaining ground. As we come to the top of that mountain cycle, we begin to move into **performing**, and God moves in us and through our relationship of perseverance. He breathes on us and things around us start shifting. We have crossed the threshold of the cycle of perseverance.

**The Kingdom of God in us moves forward because of God! His will that is implemented within our souls compels us forward in perseverance of right relationship with our Savior.** I have discovered that many people are skilled and skills are learned and can assist us forward. Gifts, talents, education and skills can advance us. But if you do not have perseverance of a commitment that is driven by relationship with Jesus, no gift, talent, or skill will see you through the lifetime journey of our calling, purpose and destiny. You will not survive the process of the seasonal cycle without surrendering to the training and persevering grace to sustain your walk of character and integrity. You were created for a purpose! You have a book in heaven written about you -- your destiny and calling to be fulfilled here on the earth. Just as the Father is faithful to keep His promises to us, we also have to be willing to die to the flesh of compromise, feelings and emotions and step into the perseverance of righteous integrity, character and obedience to see our promises fulfilled! It's the same in the Kingdom of God. There are battles with the soul, battles with the enemy, battles with people and the battle we have with God Himself! Conquering and overcoming takes a perseverance mindset.

In this journey, we must know this: no matter what experience, battle, circumstance or relational problem may occur, the question we are always to ask is, "What am I to learn from this? What aspect of the Lord am I going to learn about that I couldn't learn in any other circumstance?" Remember that when you say "yes" to Jesus and invite Him into your heart. God is in charge of your life, and at the moment you step out of Satan's domain, God now orders your steps. So I firmly believe most of all our battles are with God Himself. We just don't realize that it's Him trying to cleanse us, heal us, save us, and prevent us from greater consequences we can't understand, at the time. God is always ahead of us. He only wants what is best for us! He is a good Papa and He gives good gifts to His children. (Mat 7:11) So let us truly grasp and understand the intent of His heart is always goodness! Let us determine to trust in His goodness toward us, knowing that we are always face-to-face with Him 24/7/365 and never separated from Him. We can then boldly come to the Throne Room of grace and mercy because of the promise of the perseverance of Christ's sacrifice. (Heb. 4:16)

**The day we persevere past our self into complete, radical abandonment is the season where the promises of destiny are defined and revealed. It is only His grace that provides us the ability to persevere towards the**

## PROMISES of LIFE MORE ABUNDANTLY!

***Philippians 3:14 (NIV)***
*I press on toward the goal to win the prize for which God has called me heavenward in Christ Jesus.*

Prayer Point

Dear Papa God, give me eyes to see from heaven's perspective, from heaven to earth and not from earth to heaven. Give me Your grace to persevere and finish my race well. Holy Spirit, reveal anything that hinders my ability to persevere and finish well. (*Wait on the Holy Spirit to speak*) _____. I surrender everything that causes me to stop short and not press onto the prize of the high calling. I surrender everything. Pour out Your grace to persevere, Lord. I choose you, Jesus. Amen.

## God Loves Me

God loves me
His blessings cover me all over
With the gold of His grace
The morning's dawn of golden light
Has nothing to compare
I am awash in the love of Christ
The soft petals of His Glory
Cover me as dew
On a soft summers night

Betty Clinton
July 16, 1999

## RESOURCES

The following are helps to guide you in your spiritual journey and relationship with Jesus. They are intended for use with other believers you trust to assist you in the process of reflection, dialog, and encountering Jesus at a deeper level. James 5:16 states, *"Therefore, confess your sins to each other and pray for each other so that you may be healed."* Salvation and Baptism of the Holy Spirit is always the first step of the prayer process. We recommend that you pray these prayers out loud with a trusted leader, friend or counselor. *This is not intended as any form of therapy or counseling. It is for Biblical advisement only and we advise you to seek out trained professionals if you are in need of help. (Pray all prayers out loud.)*

### The Romans Road of Salvation

**Prayer for Salvation** (Rom 3:10, 23, 5:12, 5:8, 6:23, 10:9-10, 17, 10:13, 2 Cor. 6:2)

> Dear Lord Jesus, I confess to You, that I have sinned in (list them) _____. I confess what I remember, all I can't remember and all sins of omission. I believe that You died on the Cross and took my punishment of those sins in my place. I believe that You were born of the Virgin Mary. I believe that You were resurrected on the 3$^{rd}$ day to save humanity and reconcile me back to right relationship with my Father who created me. I surrender my life, heart, mind and

soul to You now and make You the Lord of my life. Jesus, come into my heart, heal and save me. I receive Your salvation. Thank You Jesus for the price You paid for my sin. Thank You that I am now connected to my heavenly Father just as if I had never sinned and I am now made right in His sight. God sees me now as righteous because of Your blood shed that pardoned my sin. Thank You, Jesus, for this gift. Amen

**Prayer for Baptism of Holy Spirit** (Acts 2:4, 32-33, 38-39, 10:44-46, Mk 1:8, Lk 11:13 Rom 11:29)

Dear Lord Jesus, cleanse me from all unrighteousness. I repent and renounce all occult activities and all false religions in my bloodline. I renounce all religious teachings that blaspheme the Holy Spirit saying that it is of the enemy or that it is not for today. I believe that You sent the Holy Spirit when You ascended to the Father as our Comforter and Equipper and I ask you to baptize me in the fullness of the Holy Spirit with an impartation of the fruits of the Spirit and all the gifts of the Spirit including speaking in Your heavenly languages of other tongues. (1 Cor. 14:2, 4, 15, Rom. 8:16-17, 26, Eph. 1:13, Gal. 5)

*Note: Various churches have different doctrinal viewpoints on the Baptism of the Spirit. I recommend you look for a fellowship that is Charismatic or Pentecostal in their beliefs to assist you in growing in the Spirit and gifts of the Lord.*

1. Now go and tell someone that you just received Jesus as your Lord and Savior!
2. Purchase a Bible and begin reading the book of John.
3. Find a Church or Fellowship group that believes Jesus is the Son of God and believes Heaven and Hell are real places. A place where the Bible is revered as the inspired Word of God and they believe and operate in the gifts of the Spirit.
4. Contact us and share with us what has happened to you.
info@theresmoreministries.com
FB – There's More Ministries, Inc.
Cheryl Weaver Ministries

## Breaking the Bastard Curse of 10 generations

*Deuteronomy 23:2 (KJV)*
*A bastard shall not enter into the congregation of the LORD; even to his tenth generation shall not enter into the congregation of the LORD.*

*1 John 1:9 (KJV)*
*If we confess our sins, he is faithful and just to forgive us our sins, and to cleanse us from all unrighteousness.*

1) **Confession of ancestors' bastard sin. (Jer. 14:20, Dan. 9:8, Neh. 1:6)** (Confess Prayer Out loud.) Lord, I acknowledge the iniquity of my ancestors', my mother's and my father's bloodlines. We have sinned against You. Our sin of fornication/adultery/lust out of wedlock has created this bastard curse against me and my children to 10 generations. I confess their sin and repent. I confess my sin and repent.

2) **Jesus took the curse. (Is. 53:3, Gal. 3:13-14, 2 Cor. 5:21)** Dear Lord, I place this bloodline bastard curse on the Cross now, in Jesus' name.
3) **Jesus forgives and remits confessed sins (Heb. 10:17-18, Due. 7:9)** Dear Jesus, I receive Your forgiveness of my ancestors' iniquities. choose to forgive my ancestors' sin. I choose to forgive myself, in Jesus' name. In Jesus' name, I declare these sins remitted by the Blood of the Lamb. I break the bloodline bastard curse off me and my children and my children's children to 10 generations.
4) **Jesus purifies the soul and makes perfect. (Eph. 5:26, Heb. 9:9, 12-14, 10:1-14)** I receive Your sanctification and Your cleansing of my bloodlines. I receive the bloodline promise of blessings to my descendants to 1,000 generations.
5) **Jesus restores the promise. (Gen 27, 49)** I receive the restoration of my birthright, in Jesus' name. Amen!

**<u>Generational Curse Prayer</u>** (Deut. 28:59, Ex. 20:5-6, 34:7)

This can be associated with family sin issues, healing of physical or emotional issues, or any kind of cyclical behavioral patterns or behaviors. Our personal sins can also generate a generational curse, I.e. abortion, sexual abuse.

<u>Ten Warnings of a Curse</u> – Deuteronomy 28 (Curses come from the root of someone's rebellious sins against God.

1) Dire poverty or perpetual financial insufficiency, funds, resources, unproductive land, robbery. (vs. 16-17, 29, 48)
2) Barrenness and impotency, miscarriages, abortions, and related female complications. (vs. 18)
3) Plans and projects meeting with disaster, confusion, destructive behaviors, ruin, failure, work with no results, labor in van, and loss of all favor, disdain. (vs. 19, 30, 63)
4) Death, untimely and unnatural, murder, abortion, rebellion. (vs. Gen 4:10-12, Deut. 21:18, 28:25, 45, 48, 55, 61, Mat. 15:4)
5) Sickness, fever, inflammation and diseases; especially chronic, hereditary and incurable diseases. (vs. 22, 27-28, 35, 59)
6) Life traumas; going from one crisis to another, oppression, unproductive environmental and ecological issues. (vs. 22-26, 42, 59, Gen 4:10-12)
7) Mental and emotional breakdown. (vs. 28, 32-34, 65-67)
8) Breakdown of family relationships, including divorce, not honoring parents. (vs. Due. 22:29, 27:16, 28:59, 64-65, Lev. 20:9, Mal. 2:16, Mk 10:9, Eph. 6:1-4, Prov. 20:20)
9) Accidents and accident prone. (vs. 48, 61, 65)
10) Spiritually hindered in hearing God's voice, sensing God's presence, understanding the Bible, concentration in prayer and being devoid of spiritual gifts. ( Deut. 28)

Galatians 3:13 says, *"Christ redeemed us from the curse of the law by becoming a curse for us, for it is written: 'Cursed is everyone who is hung on a tree.'"* Praying appropriates the promise to us, just like praying for salvation.

Dear Lord Jesus, I repent for my ancestors in my mom's and my dad's family lineage for the sins of _____. I ask Your forgiveness for their sins. I repent where I have fallen into the sin of _____. I ask for Your forgiveness. I renounce the sin and oppression of _____ on both my mom's and my dad's family bloodlines. I cleanse them from these sins, oppressions and generational curses now, in Jesus' name. I break these curses off my children and grandchildren to 1,000 generations as Your Word says, with the Blood of Jesus. I break these generational curses off all family members now, in Jesus' name. I ask You to reveal truth to all my family so they can walk in victory over this bondage, in Jesus' name.

I break all bondages associated with this off me and my family. I repent of any judgments that came from this sin and I break the judgments and all penalties now. I cancel the harvest of that judgment off me and my bloodlines and my children, in Jesus' name. I cancel any and all consequences in my bloodlines, breaking and renouncing all curses. I cancel all activation points of all curses, in Jesus' name.

I cover myself and my family in the blood-bought glory light of Jesus, and I receive the bloodline blessings of my family lineage! Every blessing that was not received I receive it now, in Jesus' name. (Ask Him to show you what they are, typically the opposite of the oppression) _____? Fill me with all that You have stored up in the storehouses of heaven for me and my family, in Jesus' name. Amen.

## Breaking Soul Ties

What is a soul tie? In most cases it is a tie where two souls are joined together illegitimately by making an ungodly covenant, having a dysfunctional relationship, a blood pact, tattoo pact, and sexual union with another person (outside of marriage). Through soul ties a spiritual channel is formed.

When we become married, we are as the Bible states in **Ephesians 5:31** "joined", a man is joined to his wife. And in **Matthew 19:6** regarding marriage; **"Therefore what God has joined together, let no man separate."** This is the "holy soul tie" or covenant for which this was created and intended. When we join together with other sexual partners that are not our spouse, we are creating a soul tie that affects our soul and surrendering our birthright inheritance.

**1 Cor. 6:16 - 20 (KJV)** states it like this:

> *What? Know ye not that he which is joined to a harlot is one body? For two, saith he, shall be one flesh. 17 But he that is joined unto the Lord is one spirit. 18 Flee fornication. Every sin that a man doeth is without the body; but he that committeth fornication sinneth against his own body. What? Know ye not that your body is the temple of the Holy Ghost which is in you, which ye have of God, and ye are not your own? 20 For ye are bought with a price: therefore glorify God in your body, and in your spirit, which are God's.*

### Prayer to Break a Soul Tie (Pray out loud)

Dear Lord Jesus, I repent for making a soul tie with (list their names) _____. I ask Your forgiveness for this sin and for placing them in higher esteem than You in my life, Jesus. I break all unclean associations with this person and objects now, in Jesus' name. I attach myself to the root of Jesse, Jesus Christ (Isaiah 11:1-3). I forgive myself and break the soul tie now in Jesus' name through the shed Blood of Jesus Christ. Amen.

### Prayer of Renouncement

Dear Lord Jesus, I repent for my sins of _____. I renounce all involvement with _____. I ask Your forgiveness. Your Word says that if I confess my sins, I am forgiven. I choose to forgive myself. I cover myself in the Blood of Jesus, and every area that was associated with the issue of _____. Holy Spirit, fill me with the Baptism of Your love and Spirit now, in Jesus' name.

Note: Read the Word, worship and spend time with the Lord to fill up the areas you just emptied out.

### Footsteps to Freedom (Isa. 61)

I have worked in the deliverance field for 30 years and completed deliverances with hundreds of people. I have seen the Lord bring deliverance long distance over the phone, video and text. I have personally experienced many deliverances with the Holy Spirit because there was no one who knew how to bring this type of healing to me. I have also experienced spiritual rape because I so desperately needed deliverance that I allowed myself to be alone with a man for deliverance. Don't ever allow yourself to be alone with the opposite sex in any kind of ministry setting no matter what their stature! It is not appropriate for believers and is a demonic setup for failure!

The Lord moves with a humble and surrendered heart. May what I have learned over this time assist you in your process. This information does come with a disclaimer. This is not to replace any type of professional counseling. These are simply some practical tips on how to offer and seek freedom of root issues for the broken soul. **It is always best to work with at least two people** -- a local pastor, counselor, small group leaders, seers or intercessors. (Please note: if someone has been deeply involved in abuse, occult, or satanic ritual abuse, you need to refer them to a professional counselor. It is ok, and wise, to refer people that you don't feel qualified to handle.) Scripture states, "Where two or more are gathered, there He is in the midst of them". There is wisdom in many counselors and discernment when we work together as a team. (Prov. 11:14) James 5:16 says, "That when we confess our sins one to another, we will be healed." Most of all, I would like to stress I have received deliverance in every way possible and what I most importantly want to underscore is "Love". (I Cor. 13) The Kingdom of God is Love and God is Love, and the enemy operates in the opposite commodities of fear and hate. (1 John 4:7-8, 10:10) Make sure that the love of God is your focus and that loving the individual you are ministering to is your priority! Jesus cared about each person He touched, healed, and raised from the dead. (Mk. 5:19, John 11:38:44) He had love and compassion for them. We also must exude that kind of love to have the true authority of Christ's power. Many times just the love pouring out of my eyes deep into the person's soul has brought deliverance. (Eyes are the window to the soul.) I like this acrostic to help with this.

**L** - Listen, **O** - Open up, **V** - Value others, **E** - Enjoy

Footsteps to walk in:

1) Make sure the recipient has asked Jesus into their hearts and has welcomed the Holy Spirit. (John 3:16, Act 2:34)
2) You want to make sure the person is completely surrendered and fully ready to change his or her lifestyle and/or behaviors. If they are not – STOP! If someone experiences deliverance and goes back to their old behaviors, they will receive seven times more demons and become much worse off than they started! It is ok if they are not ready. Pray a prayer of blessing and release them. Many are ready for freedom but are ashamed and/or fearful. I have learned that by sharing a vulnerable part of my testimony and assuring them that we all have sinned and fallen short of the glory of God helps them to open up and know that no one here is judging them, we're simply here to bring more of Jesus to them. Assure them this is strictly confidential.
3) Gather 1 or 2 other Christians to pray and ask God if you need to fast. (Is. 58:6, Mk. 9:29) (Depending on who the person is and what the issues are, I may ask them to fast something as well.) Make sure all parties understand that everything here is confidential and is not to be addressed or discussed outside of this prayer time. This model is one of respect for the person receiving prayer! We want them to feel loved, valued, and honored as Jesus honors. This process isn't loud, lengthy, or chaotic. There is order

and authority and it is based on loving the person to wholeness.

4) Pray and ask for wisdom and discernment and invite the Lord to orchestrate your time. (1 Cor. 12:8)

5) Invite the angels assigned to you to assist in the removal of any demons once expelled. (Heb. 1:14)

6) The enemy functions in a chain of command; in a structure format with lesser ranking demons to higher ranking demons. The lesser guard the higher. (Eph. 6:12) It is important to have **only one person** directly ministering to the person. All other people should be praying quietly and giving what information they receive to the "one designated" to minister healing and deliverance. If there are many voices and hands being laid on the person (which I have experienced many times in my early years of deliverance) it brings in confusion and allows the enemy opportunity not to engage. The enemy only responds to authority. (Which doesn't mean screaming.) Only the one ministering should be the one laying hands on and speaking to the prayee.

7) Most deliverance issues center around a lie that we have accepted as truth. (John 8:44) The goal is to get to the root issue and uncover the deception that the enemy has helped us believe in the situation. Most root issues that have turned into strongholds occur in our younger years. (2 Cor. 10:3-5)

8) If the prayee has any occult family background, this will hinder your process and usually hinders the person from receiving the Baptism of the Holy Spirit as well. Typically, I start with the occult sins first before dealing with root issues. (Due. 4:19, 18:10-13, Lev. 20:6, 1 Chon. 10:13) You can find a list of occult items to renounce at: https://www.christian-faith.com/occult-check-list/ *1

*9)* Ask the following of the person receiving questions: What seems to be the issue? When did it start? What significant events happened in life surrounding that time? When was the first time you experienced this? Do you see a repeat pattern? How was your relationship with Mom and Dad? (Ask Holy Spirit to help them remember and help you know what direction to lead with. Ask for Words of knowledge.)

    *a)* Have prayee pray verbally: *Lord Jesus, I trust You. I give You permission to come into every area of my heart and soul today. I release all control to You. I relinquish all guardianship of my heart and soul to You, Jesus. I say to any other guardians, you are no longer needed. Jesus is my guardian now. Go, in Jesus' name. (2 Chron. 16:9a, Ps. 91:7, Is. 52:12, 58:8)*

**10)** **As the prayer, it is very important to stand in proxy for the one that hurt them and tell the person "I am sorry, I was wrong for hurting, betraying, abusing, abandoning, robbing you, etc. I was selfish and wrong. Please forgive me." Note: this usually provokes a strong emotional release when done with real empathy on your part. If you don't have a release, make sure the person is truly engaged in the process and wants to receive healing and is still willing to continue. (Ezek. 22:40, Gen 50:20, Ps. 106:23, Esther 8, Gal.6:2)**

11) Periodically, reassure them throughout the process they are doing great, asking them if they are ok and you are ok to keep going.

12) Make sure the person receiving acknowledges the following verbally (Rom 10:8-11):

    *a) Forgives those who hurt them. It may take a little time. Reassure them that we are not excusing the behaviors. They are choosing to forgive as an act of obedience to Jesus. Their will and feelings will come later. (Eph. 4:31-32, 6:14-15, Luke 6:37)*

b) *Repents for their sins or sin responses. (1 John 1:9, Acts 2:38) Ask Holy Spirit to reveal anything needed to repent of.*

c) *Renounces issues of open doors, judgments, curses, vows, behaviors, idolatry, fornication, murder, addiction, etc. (You can refer to the other prayers at the end of each chapter and the resource section of the book). (James 4:7, Mat 13;18-23)*

d) *Breaks the bondages and the harvest of those bondages attached to the sin behaviors, in the name and Blood of Jesus. (Jer. 30:8,Ps.2:3 107:14, Naham 1:9,13, John 8:34, 10:10, Acts8:23, 2 Peter 2:19, Rom. 6:18, I.e. Drugs: Repens for abusing God's temple and giving your mind over to other powers besides Holy Spirit, renounce the spirit of drug usage and break the bondage of addiction. Forgive yourself. Sex: repent for having sex before marriage and breaking God's commandment and causing someone else to do the same. Renounce the spirit of lust, break the bondage of fornication, break the soul ties, and forgive.)*

e) *Accept God's forgiveness thru Jesus' shed blood. He suffered for your sin. Forgive yourself.*

13) Prayer, then command all unclean spirits to leave them. (Mark 1:23-26) If the person begins to manifest during the prayer time, stop the process. (When someone is manifesting, the demon is wanting to interfere. It is attempting to take control of the person and the situation for attention, testing your authority and to ultimately prevent eviction. Your role is to take authority calmly but firmly and bring the person back to the forefront of their soul to communicate only with them!) Look the prayee in the eyes, request they look you in the eyes, and call their name and call them to "come forward" respectfully and calmly. (Call their name, i.e. Linda come forward now in Jesus name.) "Tell the enemy he cannot manifest here and

must simply leave when you command him to." <u>To repeat, upon a manifestation do not change into other forms of deliverance or have multiple people become involved</u>. Trust Holy Spirit and simply, calmly, request the person by name to come forward, **until they consciously can say the name of Jesus and tell the demons not to manifest and remain silent.** (Luke 4:35) Request them to come forward and say, "Jesus". Demons will not say His name. This is how you know they are back in control and present with you and the demon is no longer in controlling behavior. Demons lie, so we never want to talk to demons, only the person! We are in authority over them and can calmly, but firmly, demand they not manifest including before we begin.

Then start back where you have left off. You may have to repeat this process numerous times until you have found the root issues and prayed through the above. The more you work through Step 9, the easier this step is. The more authority you know you possess, the easier the process will become for all involved. I have used the "Footprints to Freedom" process for over 25 years and the demons have to obey and come out peacefully! If you have strong manifestations, the prayee is most likely not revealing everything, ie. a sin that is an open door for the demon to remain. (They are usually afraid, ashamed, or demonically resistant. If they are unwilling, stop and seal what you have done and bless them.) Reassure them and restart back at the interview process (step 9) after you call them forward. Most of all, the Jesus in you is all the authority you need. The Blood of the Lamb overcame every demonic principality! We rejoice that our names are written in the Lamb's Book of Life!

14) As you begin to pray, there tends to be multiple issues arise. Have one of the intercessors write down all the specific issues and keep a log. Deal with one issue at a time only. When the prayee has received freedom, you can move to the next issue as the Holy Spirit leads. Don't be in a hurry and remember -- Listen, Open up, Value others and Enjoy the Lord and the prayee in the process.
15) When you feel you have finished with a root and have commanded the enemy to leave, the prayee might show signs of burping, coughing, hiccupping, sighing, yawning, stretching, or possibly puking. All parties should feel a release in the Spirit (Mark 9:20). Ask Holy Spirit if there is anything else He wants to do or reveal. Wait on Him, then follow His lead. At any given time, the intercessors can interact with you and provide information quietly to you to assist in what they are seeing and hearing in the process. Upon final prayer, seal what the Lord has done in the Blood of Jesus. (Eph. 1:13)
    a) *Upon completion, have prayee thank the Lord Jesus and begin to praise Jesus. This will be a sign they are free from the demon that you were delivering them from. (John 8:36, 2 Thes. 3:3)*
    b) *Then, if needed, repeat the process for the next issue on the log.*

Post Deliverance Instructions for Prayee – Read out loud. *(Eph. 6, 1 Cor. 10-13, Rom. 12:2, 1 Thes. 4:1-18, Ps. 91, 103:2-4, 1 John 4:1).* Explain they have experienced deliverance, which is like surgery, but on the soul. They may feel weak for a day or two. They need extra time to rest, to eat meat and to recuperate from the energy loss. (I recommend that for the prayers as well.)

    a) *Remind them they have emptied the house and now they must fill it to keep it occupied. (Mat. 12:44-45)*

b) *That the enemy will try and return in a few days or a couple of weeks. That they have authority and to renounce him and command him to leave them and silence all voices but the voice of the Father, Son and Holy Spirit. (Eph. 6, Ps. 91, 103:2-4, 1 John 4:1)*
c) *Read the Word. Mark or Proverbs is a good reference.*
d) *Fill up on worshipping and praying in the Spirit. Science has proven that if you pray in the Spirit 30 minutes a day it increases your immune system 30-40%. (\*1)*
e) *Go and sin no more. Stay in fellowship and accountability. (Acts 2:42, 1 John 1:7,)*

Please Note:

In all cases of prayer above, if you have any paraphernalia, books or objects from other religions, cults, foreign cultures, unclean relationships, and items passed from ancestors of such things, it is appropriate to destroy and/or throw the items away. Seek the Holy Spirit for His Instructions. It is recommended that you do not sell them or gain profit from the items; that will continue to keep you in bondage. It should be removed and in most cases, destroyed to prevent others harm.

If you are struggling with this, ask the Holy Spirit to reveal to you what you should do. In the meantime, place the item in the garage or outside the home temporarily until you hear from the Lord what to do. It is wise to ask believers to come over and perform a spiritual house cleaning in your home, casting out anything unclean and blessing each room with God's peace and the intention for its use.

We recommend that you discuss these prayers with Christian leaders for personal Biblical advisement and direction, or you may contact There's More Ministries, Inc. at info@theresmoreministries.com.

CHERYL CLINTON WEAVER

# REFERENCES CITED

Chapter – The Promise of Repentance

1) "Webster's Dictionary 1828 – Repent." Merriam Webster, https://www.webstersdictionary1828.com/Dictionary/repent.

Resources

Footsteps to Freedom reference to tongues:

1) Speaking in Tongues, Tongues on the Mind, Constance Holden, Nov. 2, 2006, ScienceMag.org https://www.sciencemag.org/news/2006/11/tongues-mind
2) Medical Facts about Speaking in Tongues – Carl R. Peterson, M.D. His Grace Is Enough, Believer's Identity, Holy Spirit, June 14, 2011 https://hischarisisenough.wordpress.com/2011/06/14/medical-facts-about-speaking-in-tongues-carl-r-peterson-m-d/

Thank you for your time invested in learning about God's promises and how He desires for us to taste and see that He is GOOD! Contact us and share with us what has happened to you through reading this book. Also, if you would like to purchase one for a friend or relative, you may contact us at email below.

Look for more books coming soon from Cheryl Clinton Weaver.

>*The Abuse Structure*
> What the Church and Counselors Aren't Telling You

> *The Birthright Blessing*

> *"I'm Sorry" -- Healing Words Everyone Needs to Hear*

If you would like to get more information about her ministry, contact us as follows:

www.cherylweaver.org

www.theresmoreministries.com

info@theresmoreministries.com

FB – There's More, Cheryl Weaver Ministries

CherylWeaver@ApostleWeaver

## ABOUT THE AUTHOR

### CHERYL CLINTON WEAVER

The Lord has blessed Cheryl with the ability to believe God and operate in the five-fold as a servant and minister in many of His gifts. She has been serving the Lord since her salvation in 1990. Evangelism, leadership, physical healing, emotional healing, deliverance, and operating in the prophetic are some of the gifts the Lord chooses to manifest in her life. Her heart's desire is that none should perish and to see lost souls saved, physically healed and emotionally set free so that many may come into the Kingdom and accomplish their God-given destiny.

While serving in a myriad of leadership positions for most

of her Christian walk, Cheryl and her husband Wayne have served in several churches as small group coordinators and leadership trainers. They graduated from the Church of God Ministerial Program through Lee University, where Cheryl went on to receive her Ministerial License in 2005. She resigned in 2015 after 24 years with Aglow International in several capacities. She served as President Area leader raising up over 34 works of God in the Land of Lincoln. Cheryl loves evangelism and served also as a leader over Illinois and Iowa promoting the "royal law" of James 2, "Love your neighbor as yourself." She also founded New Beginnings, a ministry for those who suffer from the trauma of Post-Traumatic Stress Syndrome regarding abortion loss.

Cheryl was ordained in 2009, and as an Apostle in 2010 with New Life World Outreach, Tampa, Florida. She has also served as a Chaplain for Marketplace Ministries providing pastoral care and ministry to secular companies and their employees since 2005. Most recently, she started There's More Ministries, a "Catalyst" Ministry birthing a Kingdom culture of personal restoration, church transformation, and community reformation.

In the past, she has owned her own business called Help for Hire -- marketing and advertising and special events. She has had a career in Marketing and Advertising working with Mall development companies. Cheryl and her husband, Wayne, were married at sea in the Gulf of Mexico in 1990. Wayne is an International Business Manager & New Product Manager; Engineer by trade.

They have a beautiful daughter named Cassia Marie who

recently finished her 10-year volleyball career and graduated from Oakland City Christian University with a Criminal Justice major.

*Cheryl Clinton Weaver, Rev.*
www.cherylweaver.org

www.ingramcontent.com/pod-product-compliance
Lightning Source LLC
Chambersburg PA
CBHW031259110426
42743CB00041B/750